To B

You're great babies!

Every Other Twin Book is Wrong: 15 Tips on Twin Pregnancy, Infancy, and Toddler Times

Carla Shelley Anderson Wardin

Evergreen Dairy Incorporated

St Johns MI 48879

First edition

Printed in the U.S.A.

ISBN 978-1-257-03233-4

When I was seven weeks pregnant, an ultrasound confirmed I was having twins. Since I found out so early, and had a lot of time on my hands, I treated the rest of my pregnancy as if I were studying for a test.

I studied the internet, books, consulted with twin moms, and joined a twin mom group. I tried to learn everything I could about having twins and babies before the big day of their arrival occurred. What did I learn? That everyone was wrong.

Take heart in knowing …

1. Twin pregnancy can be easy.

I never slept better, had nicer hair, clearer skin, bigger boobs, or more attention than when I was pregnant. It's only nine months of your entire life. Enjoy.

That's not the line you normally hear about pregnancy, but I was lucky. I didn't have any medical problems. My doctor actually said that I was boring. This is what you're aiming for – to be boring.

Let's break it down, shall we?

Month one: (Week 1-4)

Month one barely counts as a real month of pregnancy … unless you're trying to get pregnant. If you're trying, you have two weeks to obsess about every little sign that might indicate you're pregnant. You may drink alcohol and caffeine a little more, thinking it's the last time you're going to splurge. By the time you take a positive test – bam – you get to add two weeks onto your pregnancy (because you have to calculate back to your last period and count the weeks where the egg was getting ready and fertilized and implanting, and you immediately are considered one month pregnant.)

There's always the question of when you want to tell – or if you try to hide it. I like my friend's plan: "I don't think I can bear to drink fake mixed drinks. I'll just go out, drink water, and when people ask, I'll say, "Let's not talk about it for three months in case I miscarry and you feel bad for asking."

Congratulations! You're pregnant! Time to start eating more vegetables, stop drinking, start weaning yourself off caffeine, and rejoice about your new, happy secret. You will also start devouring books like these.

Month two: (Weeks 5-8)

Now you know you're pregnant. If you're having twins, you have more hormones surging through you than a woman having a single baby, so you might be even more tired or nauseous. But not in all cases.

When I was six weeks pregnant, I got nauseated for the first time. It was such an unusual feeling that I was having difficulty discerning whether it was sickness or pregnancy.

I got my answer in the following days, because it happened every day for a week. I had intense cravings - cottage cheese, burritos – and intense nausea. I tried to figure out the formula – if I ate a tiny bit every two hours, then I felt pretty okay. If I went too long without eating, I felt sick. If I ate too much in one sitting, it was like I had rocks in my stomach.

But really … it wasn't that bad. During this time, I was living in Connecticut and telecommuting for a software company in Michigan. This week fell when I was scheduled to work in headquarters in Michigan. So, instead of working in my office in my home, where I could lie on the couch with a laptop and fleece pants, I had to shower, put on makeup, clothes, and act normal at work all day.

Plus I had to do it in front of my parents, because I stayed with them for that week. I was sure my mom would notice the size of my breasts, my pudginess, my strange eating habits, and my early bedtime. My parents noticed nothing. No one at work noticed anything. So if you can hide something like this from the people you live and work with, you can tell it's not really going to be that bad.

Here's another positive note – nausea is a good sign of a healthy pregnancy. If you're not nauseous, it's not a bad sign. My mom and sister didn't have nausea and I thought I'd be the same. But when you're throwing up, just know that the reason is because your baby (or babies) are causing your hormones to churn correctly. Vomit with hope, cheer, and gusto!

At my next appointment, my doctor suggested I take a prenatal vitamin with a lot of vitamin B6, because that's known to help with nausea. I didn't want to take it, because it cost $30 a month. But two days after I started taking it, I didn't have morning sickness anymore. It was like flipping a switch. The no-puking switch. I know this won't work for all women – because if it did then morning sickness would be but a distant memory - but it's worth a shot. I thought perhaps that it was all in my head, and that the vitamins were working as a placebo. But I stopped taking them once and the nausea returned. So even if it was all in my head, it was worth shelling out the extra money.

And … this may be the month you're finding out you're having twins! Due to the fantastic technology, women barely ever find out they're going to have twins as they're giving birth. (Yes, I realize we're just one generation removed from that.) Many women still find out at the 20-week ultrasound. But some find out even earlier.

Excited? Anxious? Thinking about the size of your house? Relax. You've got months to worry about things. Let's get ready for …

Month three: (Weeks 9-13)

Month three, I started playing the 'pregnant or fat' game. If I wear this shirt, do I just look fat? Is it obvious to everyone that I'm pregnant? I also had to start focusing on my blood sugar. When you're giving nutrition to two more people, it's important to eat enough to not get shaky or dizzy.

I took a train trip to visit my brother and his family in Delaware. On the ride down there, I packed a lunch of two peanut butter and jelly sandwiches, carrots, three apples, and water. I ate and drank steadily the entire ride there. A few hours in, with much of my food eaten and much of my book read, I started to feel a little bit uncomfortable. My jeans were too tight.

I was surprised at how quickly it'd happened. Surreptitiously I unbuttoned my pants. It wasn't enough. I had to unzip them a little too. I found a hair tie in my bag and wrapped it around my button and my buttonhole to create a sort of elastic waistband.

For a girl who cares about fashion, wearing a homemade elastic waistband is awesome.

I spent the weekend with my brother Gage and his wife Serena, who was also pregnant. While I was there, Gage said, "Hey, I have to move this bed frame upstairs – will you help me? I mean, you're not pregnant."

(My husband and I had to move a washer and dryer from our basement into the upstairs right before I visited them. Obviously, my husband knew I was pregnant, so I assisted him in moving with my supportive cheering. Anytime I'd go to try and help, he would say, straining through clenched teeth, *please don't help me. I can do it.* As he half dragged, half pushed them upstairs, wrapped in a sheet and looking like a deranged Santa Claus, I really felt like I should be helping.)

While thinking of that, I wanted to disclose my pregnancy to Gage and Serena right there, but it was too soon. Instead, I pretended to help him move his bed upstairs. I barely touched it. I just gave the impression I was helping. (Sorry about your back, Gage!)

Each night after Gage and Serena went to bed I would go downstairs and quietly, ever so quietly, eat cereal. They had already fed me three meals and dessert, but I was just so hungry! I didn't want them to think I was a pig. Even though I was. When I left, I asked them if they minded if I packed myself a lunch. I made one pb&j while they were in the room, then quickly made two more when they were with their daughter.

So, other than eating a lot of someone else's groceries, and causing possible back strain, keeping a new pregnancy secret wasn't that difficult.

Month four: (Weeks 14-17)

Finally – the first trimester is over! You've heard your baby's heartbeat, your miscarriage chances are slim, and you're starting to tell everyone … if they haven't already guessed.

Kris and I went to tell his grandpa that I was pregnant. He said, "I knew it. Your face was just beautiful and glowing." We told Kris' grandma and she said, "I thought I saw a tummy on you." Guess which response I preferred? Guess which one was true?

As I entered my second trimester, I'd gained 10 pounds. One of the definite perks of being pregnant is eating – I ate things I hadn't eaten in years.

It's difficult when you don't know how pregnancy is supposed to feel. One day, I got concerned about how my stomach felt. It felt like my uterus was pulling downward. Were these little five ounce babies in trouble? I called the doctor's office, and they were not concerned. They told me to drink water and put my feet up. It went away the same day. I assume they get these types of calls constantly and roll their eyes at each other as they're on the phone. ("*She said she was having some feelings in her uterus! A pregnant woman! I know, can you imagine?!*") That doesn't mean you shouldn't call … you should. Just remember that you're the quadrillionth person to give birth, and in most cases, everything will be just fine.

This is probably the month where you'll start looking in the mirror at your stomach and crying from happiness. (After you have the babies, you'll do the same thing, but usually only during swimsuit season.)

Month five: (Weeks 18-21)

I felt the babies move for the first time at week 17. I'd read what it felt like for babies to move – romantic and sweet images like butterflies or bubbles popping, or more realistic ones like gas. But to me, it felt exactly like what it was – a baby moving inside of you. You'll know it when you feel it. There's no mistaking it for something else.

The pregnancy books write that you should not add new stressors when you're pregnant. Especially don't start a new job or move. I was doing both. Luckily, this was by choice, so it wasn't a trying time.

We lived in Connecticut, but Kris and I had decided to buy my parents' dairy farm in Michigan. We were moving into the 130-year-old farmhouse. My parents were building a new house down the road, but it wasn't quite done yet. So, for a month, we were all going to live together. With all of our two houses' worth of possessions. Does this sound like a good way to break up a marriage and make your parents hate you, too?

I was going to start working full-time at TechSmith, a software company near our house. I'd telecommuted for them for years, and was now going to work in the office.

As a result, I had to wear clothes that were office-appropriate. I'd borrowed many from friends, and I complained to my mom about some too-short pants.

"Preggers can't be choosers," she replied.

In my new home, that was like walking through a maze of boxes, separated from my husband, who was moving a month after me, at my new job in my new office … there I was, five months pregnant.

Perhaps your five month mark will not be as action-packed. Perhaps you'll be focused on more internal matters. For my part, I was happy to have the distraction from surfing the internet all day and analyzing every single thing about my babies and my cervix. Happy to not feel the need to exercise, since I was supposed to be sitting and working eight hours a day! Happy to have easy access to restaurants and people who wanted to dine there also.

One pregnant woman's stressor is another one's diversion.

&&&&

Your 20 week point is also the time you'll most likely get an extensive ultrasound. Some offices offer a 3-D ultrasound, which I highly recommend. (Unless you, personally, have to pay for it. Then I would recommend going to see a 3-D movie instead.)

I didn't find out the sexes of my babies and so it was really interesting to see the babies' faces and try to discern whether they were boys or girls. They mostly looked skinny … and exactly the same as when they came out. I did think one of my boys was a girl, though, but hey – it's hard discerning sex from the shape of a skull.

You've had the ultrasounds. You've had the appointments. You can feel the babies moving. Things are really seeming real. You may have other experiences that factor in … not only are you having one baby – you're having two.

I went to visit a friend the night before she had her baby. Our pregnant bellies were the same size. She then delivered a 9.4 pound girl. I looked at my own stomach and wondered how much bigger it could get. I visited the newborn baby and she peed on me. I managed not to toss her across the couch, thus qualifying me as a parent, but what if it were poop? Unsure.

&&&&

Since I worked all day, and didn't nap, I slept soundly every night. If I ever woke up I'd think 'I have to get up for work in the morning,' and I'd roll over and go back to sleep. I rarely woke up to go to the bathroom. I know this is a common problem for a lot of pregnant women, but apparently the babies weren't pressing on my bladder. That, or living in a house with one bathroom which is on a different floor is enough of a deterrent to make one wait until morning.

Month six (Weeks 22-26)

This is the point when I started having Braxton Hicks contractions. They weren't at all painful, but they were worrisome. In my case, exercise seemed to bring them on. I was still walking every day and if they started when I was doing it, I just stopped. I felt almost like I could control them by sitting down and drinking water. Adversely, if they happened when I was sitting at work, I felt like I could make them subside by walking around. Probably, I didn't have any control over them anyway, but it was nice to feel like I did. I read about them online to reassure myself that they were just my body preparing itself for labor. I didn't want it to prepare itself so well that I went into labor. I called my doctor and he suggested I have a fetal fibronectin (fFN) test done.

The fetal fibronectin is another one of those modern medicine discoveries that amazes me. Fetal fibronectin is a protein that attaches the amniotic sac to the uterus' lining. It's present one to three weeks before labor begins. If you're between 24-34 weeks pregnant, the doctor takes a (painless) swab from your cervical canal. If they find the protein, there's a chance that you'll go into premature labor. If they don't find it, then there's a good chance you won't go into labor for the next two weeks. (Fewer than 5% of women with a negative fFN test deliver in the next two weeks.)

I tested negative for it, so it gave me two more weeks of non-worrying time. The Braxton-Hicks contractions were just that – false contractions.

Or as my very-good-friend Aimee said, "I know you won't go into early labor. Haven't you seen the Discovery Channel? No one cute has problem pregnancies."

Not true, but nice to hear when you're a huge, pregnant girl, buying her first D-cup bra. Seriously.

Not only will your breasts enlarge to a staggering (some might say impressive?) size, but your stomach may be so big that it feels difficult to hold up for long periods.

Since we'd just moved, this time in our life required a lot of trips to stores like Home Depot. Home Depot, to me, is like a punishment when I'm feeling my best. When we shopped, if Kris paused to look at anything for more than 30 seconds, I'd get all fidgety and immediately fatigued and would sit wherever there was room for me. Kris kindly suggested I use the wheelchairs in the stores, and I took him up on it. Everyone is really, really nice to you when you're in a wheelchair. We had people coming out of the woodwork to assist us. I was happier because my stomach didn't feel heavy, and Kris was happy because he could browse for up to two minutes before I started sighing.

Month seven (Weeks 27-30)

By the seventh month, your babies will be quite active. Doctors emphasize counting kicks – like ten a day - to make sure your baby or babies are fine. I could hit that in under ten seconds.

Though I felt great, I apparently looked bigger than I felt. I went to a twin moms meeting and was greeted with, "You're getting soooo big!" "You're huge!" "You look so uncomfortable!"

I was so annoyed. I wanted to point out to them that they had all had twins, they had been this big, and most importantly, that I was wearing pants I'd bought when I was 20 years old.

I was lucky enough that many friends passed down their maternity clothes to me. However, my stomach stuck straight out. I never once found a pair of pants or shorts that fit over my stomach. I pushed everything under my stomach, which is why I could still wear normal pants. A friend gave me some of her maternity clothes and I had to return all of them to her … I couldn't fit them over my chest, let alone my stomach. I was also fortunate to be pregnant in a time when maternity-type (empire-waisted) shirts were the style, so cheap shirts were available anywhere.

This month, I also had a momentous ultrasound. The babies were moving all around, and I had a great time watching them. As I walked out of the office, looking intently at the pictures they'd printed, I felt an overwhelming rush of love. "I *love* them!" I whispered to myself.

A (unsentimental) friend of mine and his wife had an unplanned baby. He put it to me like this: "When we told people we were going to have a baby they said, oh, your life's going to change, and I was like, yeah, yeah. Then we had her and I was like, yeah, she's a baby, yeah, yeah. And then one day she looked at me and smiled and … that was it. They were right."

I think this happens to women far earlier than it does for men. I always wanted my babies, but at one point I loved them as babies, not just as ideas of babies. When I met them, it was as if I already knew them.

I continued to be active – working, gardening, attending a bachelorette party at a bar, working on our new house. Near the end of the month, on a day I felt particularly good, a coworker told me that I looked 'downtrodden.' We teased him mercilessly about how he didn't know how to talk to girls, I once again told everyone how good I felt, and a friend happened to snap a picture of me at work. I looked at it and … I was huge. And looked tired. And downtrodden. My outside did not match my inside.

I got home that day and my mom greeted me with, "You look cute!" Demonstrating … it's important to surround yourselves with people who tell you what you want to hear.

Month eight (Weeks 31-35)

Time to get working on that baby registry, because people want to shower you with gifts! I consulted my friends and family on the registry and they gave me lots of good tips - not just items, but brands too. You can also log onto your friends' online registries to copy them.

I didn't enjoy registering for things. I'm a minimalist at heart, and the idea of my house being stuffed with THINGS was disheartening. I didn't want any of that crap; I just wanted my babies. Take along someone who isn't as emotionally attached as you are to your living space, such as your husband, your mom, or a friend who likes to buy cute stuff.

I spent a lot of this month scraping wallpaper, preparing rooms for painting, and in one memorable night, removing all the carpet in our downstairs.

Capable. Strong. Accomplished. My house was getting in order, ready for two more people to live there. On the day I reached the 34 week mark, I was thrilled. My doctor had told me that reaching 34 weeks with twins was a bronze, 36 was a silver, and 38 was a gold. I was going to be a medalist, no matter what! I was congratulating the babies (and myself) when I looked in the mirror. And stopped.

What was that on my stomach? Stretch marks?

"I'm ruined!" I yelled to my husband.

I started taking my non-stress tests at the doctor's office to evaluate the state of the babies. The nurse puts three monitors on you – one for each baby's heartbeat, and one for uterine contractions. You're hooked up to a machine that charts the three of you. They like to measure the babies' heart rates while they're at rest and while active. Not as much fun as an ultrasound, but still a nice connection to your babies.

In my 35th week of pregnancy, my mom and I went to a parade of homes in the area. Every time we walked into one of the homes, the tour guide would say, "You're not going to have that baby in here, are you!?" I told them all, "No – not until next month!" It made me laugh. When a woman held a door for me and looked at me in unmasked horror, I whispered to my mom, "It's as if people have never seen a pregnant woman before." She whispered back, "By the time women look as pregnant as you, they usually can't walk around."

Month nine (Weeks 36-40)

My doctor's office first scheduled me to deliver in week 36, but I told them I'd rather wait until week 38. As long as you and your babies are fine, there's no reason you need to deliver early. My entire pregnancy was focused on NOT having them early, so we scheduled a c-section at 38 weeks (technically 37 weeks and 5 days, due to my doctor's schedule).

You don't have to have a c-section when you have twins. My babies were breech. They'd been in the breech position for several weeks, so I didn't want to attempt a vaginal birth. My doctor wasn't against me trying, but he thought that the c-section would "take out a lot of variables." I didn't want to have one baby vaginally and one by c-section (which is rare, but still can happen). My doctor did say, "If you do decide to give birth vaginally, I do suggest you get an epidural, because after Baby A comes out, I just reach up and grab Baby B."

I liked his honesty. That's clearly an event that invites heavy drugs.

Ultrasound technicians do their very best, but it must be really hard to gauge the size of unborn babies mashed together. Ten days before mine were born, they measured Baby A as 5.13 and Baby B at 6.6. My doctor wondered aloud if I was going to break the weight record in the hospital for twins. (In reality at birth, they were 5.11 and 5.13.)

What will the ninth month bring for you? I sat down a lot. The week before I gave birth, I got an itchy rash on my stomach. I watched a DVD on how to calm crying babies, I watched a video on spinal blocks, and I read a book on sleep-training babies. So, I was continuing my studies to get ready for the rest of my life as a parent.

Luckily – and I do attribute it to a lot of luck – there was no bed rest, no premature labor, no distressed babies … very little heartburn, fatigue, or sickness. Just an easy, enjoyable pregnancy. Even though I might not have looked bouncy, I felt great right until the day I walked into the hospital to deliver them. So don't fear that your twin pregnancy is a nine-month sentence. Hopefully, you'll be incredibly, insufferably boring.

2. No matter how tough you are, you have to deal with things out of your control.

Maybe you had a problem pregnancy and delivering was a huge relief, because now they get the medical attention they need. Or they came too early and they need to stay in the hospital. Or nothing was wrong at all … until you delivered.

That's the category I fell into. After a successful pregnancy, I had a crummy aftermath.

My first suggestion is that you deliver in a hospital with a neonatal intensive care unit (NICU), preferably a level 3 unit, which is designated for infants who need "acute and complex intervention." If you don't, and your baby or babies have to be in a NICU, you will be in a different hospital from them. There was seemingly no reason why my baby would have to be in a NICU, but I wanted to avoid this situation. Believe me, it was bad enough being two floors away from him. You might want to also go and tour the facility so that if your baby does end up there, it won't seem so foreign.

Even though my babies were born at full term for twins, in an uncomplicated c-section, at healthy birth weights, Cole stopped breathing two hours after he was born. And again. And again. And six times again that night.

He was initially fine when he was born. He was crying lustily and cried most of the two hours the four of us spent together in what they call the recovery room. The recovery room was a small room with a curtain around it. A nurse was just outside to monitor the babies and me. When they took us to my hospital room, they took the babies away to give them a bath … and only brought Ty back.

This didn't fit into my plan at all. As I ticked off the weeks of pregnancy to reach the end, I thought I'd escaped the NICU stay. When I went to see him that night, it was just as I'd feared. My tiny, skinny baby was in an incubator, away from me.

We were still pretty lucky. Cole was ultimately diagnosed with 'immature breathing', meaning that he was just born too early. But before they were able to give us that diagnosis, they had to rule out anything they could think of that was wrong with him, including asking Kris and me if we were "in any way related." (Though the word 'no' immediately burst out of me, Kris shot me a questioning glance. I still bring this up and laugh about it. Kris said he just wanted to be sure before he answered.) To rule out anything, it meant numerous painful tests, pokes, and tubes for Cole.

It also meant that I had five nightmarish days ahead of me. My family was very helpful, but they couldn't be there – and I wouldn't ask them to be – around the clock.

So while I was in the hospital, here was my schedule, as I had to feed them every three hours:

- Nurse Ty.
- Pump for Cole.
- Order cafeteria food to be delivered to my room.
- Drop Ty off at the nursery on the way to the elevator. Walk to the NICU, which was three floors and several hallways away, shuffling and hunched over in pain from the surgery and because it was a weekend and there were no wheelchairs or anyone to deliver me there.
- Get to the NICU floor exactly one hour after nursing Ty to hit Cole's scheduled nursing time. Nurse Cole and deliver my pumped milk.

- Psyche myself up for the journey back downstairs. Pick up Ty at the nursery.
- Return to my room, eat my food, and set my alarm for one hour later.
- Sleep the hour until my alarm went off, and start over again, nursing Ty.

I want to stress that this is what my schedule was for *24 hours a day*. When you're taking care of a sick baby, a well baby, and yourself post-surgery, it really seemed like a lot. But what else was I to do? I wanted to nurse them both. I wanted to be with both of them. They depended on me.

I was discharged from the hospital two days before Cole was, so both days Ty, Kris, sometimes my mom and I spent the entire two days there to be with him.

This was a production in and of itself. Nurse Ty, get Ty into the car, travel to the hospital, get a report on Cole, who I hoped with every ounce of my being made it through the night without me. Sit beside Cole and nurse him. Go into a nursing room with Ty and nurse him. Eat some food with Kris. Have my mom or Kris take Ty because siblings aren't allowed in the NICU for all the hours of the day. Wish I could sleep somewhere, but the only rooms available are common rooms, and there were other mothers in there. Continue 12 hours until we had to go home. Luckily, that was for only two days – it was harder being separated from Cole than it was being in the hospital. When I was home with Ty at night I had to pump after nursing him so I could take milk back to Cole … and there was never enough.

It was a trying time. People talk about how scared they are the first night they're home from the hospital with their baby or babies, because they seem so fragile and there are no nurses to call for help.

The first night both my babies were home, Cole had already been hooked up to monitors for five days. I had no worries about his breathing. Ty seemed happy to have someone to snuggle with in his bassinet. I slept sounder that night than I had ever since they'd been born. Finally – we were all home.

Whew! Done with the deep life and death stuff, eh?! My basic advice is – even when everything looks rosy, your baby's lungs might not work. So aim to have your baby in a place with good monitors and even better nurses.

&&&&

The day after I delivered, I checked out my stomach. It had not snapped back into place as the fairy tales went – like my mom, who wore her regular clothes home from the hospital after each of her three children. I wasn't counting on that … but I wasn't counting on what I saw, either.

My stomach was a cone shape. From my sternum to below my belly button, it formed a triangle. I didn't like the looks of it. Since it was the weekend and my doctor was gone, I asked a resident about it. She checked it out and said, "Often when women have twins, their stomach muscles don't come back together. You also appear to have a hernia. If it's a hernia, and it becomes strangulated, it's life-threatening. So, it's either nothing, or it could be life-threatening."

It was really a blow. I tried not to cry, because crying engaged my stomach muscles, and they were busy healing from the surgery. So I sort of heaved and clutched my sides, trying to control my post-partum emotional response to hearing that I MIGHT DIE.

Kris comforted me, saying, "Carla, she doesn't know what she's talking about. No doctor tells you that something is life-threatening and then leaves the room. Just wait until your doctor gets back."

I was able to put it out of my mind (since I was busy tending to the babies, see previous schedule) for two days until Dr. Roth came to see me. I told him what the other doctor had said and criticized her bedside manner. He agreed. He examined me and said gently, "You've been hit hard by the pregnancy stick." He told me I had diastasis recti, which is when your stomach muscles fail to come back together after pregnancy. He said it may heal on its own, or it may require corrective surgery someday. He said, "You were very skinny and you had two large babies. Your stomach had a lot of stretching to do." He said it would probably take a year to heal.

I considered it to be a pretty good deal for two babies.

A year later, after doing lots of exercises designed just for diastasis recti, it was pretty much the same. A year after that, it was perhaps a tad smaller, but I also developed an umbilical hernia. An umbilical hernia is when part of the intestine protrudes through a weak spot in the abdominal muscles, in this case, the bellybutton. It basically looks like I have an outie bellybutton.

Now, you're wondering if this is going to happen to you, now that you're pregnant with twins. Chances are, it's not going to. First of all, have you even heard of these terms before?!

There are tips for preventing diastasis recti while you're pregnant, but they're things that few women do when they're pregnant anyway, like: Avoid wearing tight-fitting belts. (What pregnant woman wears a belt? I can just imagine – "Oooh! Look at the new maternity belt line!" They'd have to be 8 feet long!) Avoid aggressive ab workouts after 12 weeks. (Isn't pregnancy a reason to stop doing sit-ups?) Don't lift heavy objects. (Consider this a nine-month pass.)

There isn't any way to prevent umbilical hernias, but you can get them surgically repaired. If they don't hurt, though, you can just live with your new bellybutton shape.

My vanity was injured, yes. My body was not the same, no. But it's difficult to grow two people inside of you at the same time and emerge without a mark. Do I spend a lot of my time sucking in? Yes. Do I avoid tight shirts? Yes. Would I anyway? Probably.

But again, I'm the exception. You can look around at mothers everywhere and see women who did snap back into place. As long as no one tells you 'it could be life-threatening,' just try to enjoy your new baby and worry about your body later.

&&&&

While my inside was healing, my outside was burning.

Five days before I delivered I noticed a rash on my stomach. It was PUPPP, which is – no wonder they use an acronym, because the name itself is vomit-inducing - pruritic urticarial papules and plaques of pregnancy. Translated, that means itchy red rash from hell.

Since the rash is considered harmless to the mother and baby – a few sources indicated it happens to 1% of women – it isn't considered to be a big problem, except for women who want to sleep. Its cause is still unknown, but since 70% of the women who have PUPPP give birth to boys, a popular hypothesis is that testosterone is a skin irritant. (Insert your own joke here about it being an all-around irritant.)

Everything I read agreed on one point – that the only surefire cure was delivery, when the rash would go away.

After surgery they patched me up with what was, essentially, a giant piece of stretchy Velcro that covered my torso. When I took it off to shower, I saw that I had clear blisters on my stomach.

The next day, I noticed the itchiness was intensifying, and it was worst where the girdle wasn't touching – at the bottom. I'd had poison ivy numerous times, and with that, you at least get the satisfaction of scratching it. This was beyond that – it hurt to touch it.

The last thing I wanted to do was check myself out in the mirror. But during one precious break between feeding babies where I intended to sleep, I couldn't because my skin itched so horribly. I felt like I was on fire.

I got up some courage and ventured to the mirror to take a look at myself … and was horrified. My lower back, bottom, and thighs were absolutely covered with a bright red poison ivy-like rash. In most places, there weren't even individual welts – they'd all melded together so that my skin was one giant welt. One giant itching-like-mad welt.

I showed it to a nurse, expecting her to scream and alert the proper authorities, but she just gave me hydrocortisone cream in a teeny, tiny tube. I used the entire thing on the first application. It was like trying to put out a fire with a drop of water. I knew I needed something stronger, like perhaps acid.

I showed it to my doctor. He was perplexed, and gave me a prescription for an anti-histamine. Nothing. It itched as bad as ever, and seemed to be spreading.

At night while I lay in bed I told myself it was mind over matter, and I didn't have a rash, and it for sure didn't itch. My mind then told me I was stupid.

The next day, I called Dr. Roth's office and begged them to give me something stronger. This required that I walk to their office which, although attached to the hospital, was really, really far away. I went there gingerly, trying not to jar my insides or touch any fabric to my skin.

When I got there and showed the nurse practitioner, she did a double take, then called in two other nurses to look at the sideshow I'd become.

After checking to make sure it was fine for a nursing mother, she prescribed me a steroid.

Over time, the rash moved outward – my stomach cleared, and it moved down my legs and onto my arms and a little onto my face. Seven weeks later, it was completely gone.

Yes, you read that right – SEVEN WEEKS. So, technically, it did disappear after delivery, but not until much, much later.

There are many homeopathic remedies on the internet, such as drying soaps. There are more medical ones, such as steroid creams and anti-histamines.

In my case, it was time. Time to get all that testosterone irritant out of my system.

&&&&

Whew – the babies and I were home. I'd been fit before I got pregnant, and while pregnant, I'd gained 45 pounds. I didn't think recovery was going to be too big of a deal.

It wasn't horrible. I started running again when they were six weeks old, but I also had to ask Dr. Roth at my six-week checkup, "When am I going to stop wanting to take a Motrin every day?" (It tapered off. In the hospital I took it every six hours. When I went home, I took it less and less frequently, until it was one a day, usually at the end of the day when I was tired and achy.)

"I don't know," the doctor said. "I mean, I want to take one every day."

The first week home was the worst. Obviously, you're recovering from someone cutting you open and taking out a baby. You're not getting a ton of sleep. You're not going to feel the best you've felt in your life. It felt like my insides were swishing all around. It hurt to ride in a car, because every time we hit a bump I felt like my intestines and organs were coming out.

I couldn't even bear to look at the Velcro-piece they'd given me after surgery. In fact, after I washed it, I threw it on my dresser and it fell between the dresser and the wall. I didn't fish it out until years later. That's how much I disliked it.

However, I did feel that I needed support. I also wanted to wear non-maternity clothes. So I enlisted my 21-year-old sister-in-law to go and buy me a girdle.

"A … what?" she asked.

"A girdle. Basically, I want a piece of elastic that covers my torso, with bra clasps, to suck me in. I'm sure you can find one at Wal-Mart, cheap."

She came home with two. I wore the heck out of those things. It was July, yes, so it was warm, but it was better than wearing Velcro. As an added benefit, I could also wear different clothes.

So, take your time recovering, take your pain medication, and buy a girdle before you deliver so you don't have to ask a tiny young thing to do it for you.

3. Nursing is even harder than they say it's going to be.

Books emphasize that the mother needs to be dedicated to the idea of nursing. But even to someone who's completely dedicated to it, it's really hard. (Fortunately, it's also really worth it. But you won't believe that while your nipples are crying.)

Small, young babies sometimes have difficulty nursing because their suck reflex isn't developed as well as a full-term baby. Even though they were considered full-term for twins, my babies had a tough time learning how to nurse. I was so dedicated to teaching them that I didn't want them to have bottles, because I was afraid if they did, they wouldn't learn how to breastfeed.

The lactation specialist at the hospital gave me a tool called a finger feeder for Ty. A finger feeder is a tiny tube attached to a tiny plastic cylinder. So you pump, pour your milk into the container, place the tube on your finger, and let the baby suck on your finger. When he sucked on it, he got milk and hopefully, the idea of sucking. As an added bonus, Kris could feed Ty. We did this with Ty for the first day, as well as trying to nurse.

Cole, even though he was in the NICU, was a little better at nursing than Ty. I was also pumping milk for him in the beginning. The NICU nurses asked me if we wanted Cole to have a tube that went into his nose down to his stomach to feed him milk, or if I wanted them to feed him a bottle. Again, since I was afraid he wouldn't learn to nurse, I opted for the tube feeder.

That's right, you've got it so far. The totally-dedicated-to-nursing mom is still nursing, but the babies are really drinking pumped milk out of tubes.

Eventually, the NICU nurses told me that Cole would have to be able to nurse enough or drink from a bottle before they felt comfortable sending him home. Then, we would engage in a stressful exercise - the weigh-in.

They would strip Cole, then put him on a scale. Then after I nursed him, they'd weigh him again to see how much milk he got. If he had gained a few ounces, I would rejoice. One time, he actually lost weight after he ate. The nurse eyed me suspiciously. So perhaps those scales aren't right every time.

It was stressful - pumping, nursing, and feeding two babies separately every three hours (ALL NIGHT LONG TOO) in the hospital.

Since breastfeeding is considered healthy for babies, I thought I was going to have a ton of support. I fondly remember nurse Yvonne coming into my hospital room and waking me during one of my precious hours of sleep. She shook me awake, gestured to Ty beside me and said, "He is not getting enough. You need to feed him formula." I scrambled for the paper they'd given me to keep track of their feedings. (It looks like it was written by an insane person, the way I'd scribbled on it.) I said, "I fed him three hours ago!" She looked at my paper and said, "You need to write more clearly. And he's sleeping too much. You need to feed him more. Maybe a bottle."

While I realize she was trying to do what was best for Ty, my goodness, I disliked her. But her insistence made me even more determined. I said firmly, "I'm *trying* to teach him how to breastfeed."

I also asked if the hospital's lactation specialist could come and help me. Before they were born, I'd researched, looked at pictures, talked to friends … all on how to help the baby latch well. But until she helped me, I realized that Ty wasn't really latching on well at all.

It's important that one be prepared for a lactation specialist. First of all, your breast is exposed. Second of all, she will grab onto it and stuff it into your baby's mouth. Third, you will hardly believe how wide your baby's mouth will open, and the whole thing seems a little impossible because the baby's nose is smashed into your skin.

Don't get me wrong – it was incredibly helpful. Showing is always better than telling, right?! Even if you're half-naked.

After she showed me and I had a successful feeding with Ty, I asked the lactation specialist if she could come around for the next feeding. She gently told me that she had to see every new mother in the hospital and she wouldn't be able to come back again for my entire hospital stay. While I completely understand that I wasn't the only patient in the hospital, this made me panicky. What if I couldn't do it again?!

There was a lactation specialist in the NICU as well. I made an appointment with her, and due to my babies' troubles, she suggested I use nipple shields. They're soft, plastic caps that fit over your nipples. When the babies suck, the nipples pool with milk and it makes it easier for them to drink.

I tried them, and they actually worked really well. I could also actually see that milk was being expelled. But I scoffed a bit. "Women have been breastfeeding since the beginning of time! Why shouldn't I be able to do it without this piece of plastic?" I asked, feeling silly that I needed a tool.

"Women have also been using devices to try and make it easier since the beginning of time," she said. "Archeologists have unearthed what they believe are stone nipple shields."

Primitive women had so much trouble breastfeeding that they manipulated stone to assist them? I took the plastic nipple shield. I figured it was my duty, seeing as it had been through many, many product improvements.

&&&&

By the time we left the hospital, with the assistance of the nipple shields, the boys were nursing fine.

It was time for their first feeding at home. I decided I might as well get off to a good start – feeding them both at the same time.

This was another piece of information I'd gleaned from my research. Nursing two babies is a time-consuming, so if you fed them at the same time, you'd have twice as much!

Here's the background – I planned on breastfeeding the boys exclusively. My husband was running our family farm, so I told him I didn't expect him to get up in the night. He had to run heavy machinery during the day, so I wanted him to be alert. And he wasn't going to be able to feed them anyway. As a result, for my first dual-feeding, I didn't want his assistance.

First, I took my shirt off and put on my nipple shields. I picked Ty up out of the bassinet and placed him on the recliner. I picked up Cole and placed him beside him. I took two pillows and managed to manipulate myself between them. I tried to hold their heads and move them toward me to latch on. Their little hands would randomly knock off the shields. They were crying. I started to cry. Kris stood in front of me, watching and trying to offer assistance. Like a crazy person, I said, "Don't help! You won't be here at 3am *in the morning*!" He backed off, scared.

With some luck, I got both of their heads positioned correctly and they ate. I put them back in their bassinet and they fell asleep. I headed to take a shower, and as I passed them, I didn't feel that normal rush of love and wonder. Instead, I was filled with complete and utter dread for the next feeding.

In the shower, I came to a realization. These babies couldn't even hold their heads up! I didn't HAVE to feed them at the same time! Sure, it would take longer, but it would also not make me fear them! It was an incredible relief.

So that's what I did. I fed them individually, every three hours, for the next week. I often had to wake Ty up and keep him awake as I fed him. Cole was always hungry at the three-hour point. I thought it was ridiculous and sort of mean that I had to feed them that often, but they were small – 5.4 and 5.5 when we left the hospital.

A week after I brought them home, I took them to the doctor to get weighed. In one week of feeding them every three hours (EVEN AT NIGHT), Cole had gained two ounces. Ty weighed exactly the same.

I was depressed. Eight times a day. Seven days a week. A crummy two ounces?!

The doctor was a little concerned and asked me to bring them back in five days.

I was tired, but their lack of weight gain made me even more determined to help them grow. The next day, I took off the nipple shields and fed on demand. Basically, that meant anytime they cried, I'd feed them. It was exhausting, so I went back to the three-hour schedule.

At the second weigh-in, Ty had gained six ounces and Cole had gained eight. Ah! Finally, the pay-off for having people manipulate my boobs, criticize my record-keeping, and listen to my instructions not to help me! It was beginning to feel worth it. I felt like I was on my way to big, fat babies.

&&&&

By the time they were a month old I was able to start feeding them simultaneously. It didn't happen as part of a plan, but out of pity.

One afternoon, Ty awoke first, so I started feeding him. Five minutes into it, Cole awoke and started screaming. Screaming. He was hungry and I felt bad for him. However, I couldn't make Ty quit, because then he'd cry. I slithered off my chair and onto the floor, Ty still attached. With one arm, I moved Cole off of his chair and latched him on. I was doing it. Out of necessity, I was doing it. I fed them in tandem for the rest of my nursing days.

&&&&

When the boys were six weeks old, my nipples began hurting. And by hurting, I mean that when the boys latched on it was as if there were shards of glass being shoved into me. It hurt even to have material touch me. It hurt so much I'd cry.

"It hurts so much," I told Kris as I cradled them on the couch. "I just want to rip their heads off and throw them across the room."

"I really, really wish you'd stop saying that," he said.

I tried everything suggested in books. (Lansinoh lotion, compresses, making sure I was getting a good latch, I'd quit using the nipple shields and tried using them again.) I thought perhaps the pain was being caused by an infection – something horrible, like a yeast infection. I went to my general practitioner and told him of my fears.

He examined me and said, "You don't have an infection. You're just . . . how can I put this . . . overused. You're nursing two babies all day and have been for weeks. Carla, really, by three months babies can make their own antibodies. Don't feel like you have to breastfeed them if it hurts this much."

He suggested that I try pumping and feeding them with bottles, since that might give my skin a break. That night, we took the boys to a baseball game and fed them formula for the first time. They sucked it down, not even seeming to notice it was anything different. I decided I'd just pump later that night.

I had a nice pump. But by the time I went to pump that night, my breasts were rock hard. I placed the pump on and the suction immediately caused my nipple to bleed. It hurt as much, if not more, than the babies. I decided to just skip that feeding.

It turned out that was a bad idea. My breasts hurt so much I couldn't sleep, and I got a fever. I was tired and in pain and had to take care of two people who were hurting me. The next day, I never changed out of the tank top and shorts I slept in AND RECEIVIED VISITORS.

From that day on, I fed them one bottle of formula a day. That seemed to be the magic number for us. It gave my breasts a 6-hour break, and as an added bonus, I gave them the bottle when we were out. That cut down on the amount of times I had to nurse them at the same time in the backseat of our car. (Yes, I could have done it separately, but when you're nursing in a car, it's better to get it done as fast as possible. The air conditioning had to be running in the summer. What am I, made of money?!)

For the first month, I slept on the couch in our living room with the babies in a bassinet beside me. It was easier for me because our house only had one bathroom, and I always wanted to wash my hands after I changed a baby, so the amount of stairs would have been hard in the beginning.

When I moved back to my bedroom and put them in their room, feeding them in the middle of the night went like this: I'd pick them up at the same time in my arms and carry them downstairs, really concentrating on not tripping. I'd place them on the couch sit in between them. After I fed them I'd gather them up, mount the stairs and place them back into their crib.

I thought fondly of how my friends would tell me that nursing their babies would put them to sleep. I imagined them gently placing a sleeping baby in his bed. This seldom worked in our case. The gathering and the jostling made them alert, but on the plus side, they learned how to put themselves to sleep fairly early.

&&&&

Even through breastfeeding was hard, a reason I was able to continue doing it is that no one ever pressured me. For instance, at my six-week checkup after delivery I told my obgyn that nursing was hard.

"Well … you don't have to breastfeed," he said. "They're making their own immunities by now."

I told my mom I didn't like breastfeeding. She was silent, not giving me her opinion either way. I took that to mean that I could do whatever I wanted.

I told my husband. He said, "Whatever you want is fine with me."

I told my friends that it was hard. They readily agreed.

But by the time I got through the beginning, and then started giving them a bottle a day, not nursing them seemed like I did a lot of work for nothing. And it did get easier. Eventually, I could nurse them at the same time anywhere … in the previously-mentioned parked cars, on floors, on beds, etc.

When they started eating at six months, they understandably became less interested. I also thought that perhaps they might be hungrier, so at seven months I started supplementing with a bottle at night. So I was now nursing them, feeding them food, and giving them two bottles a day.

By the time they were nine and a half months, I was nursing them when they woke up and at night. I went to feed Ty in the morning and he looked at me like I was crazy – GET THAT OUT OF MY FACE. He acted like he'd never nursed before in his life and he had no idea what I was doing. Cole nursed three days longer and then gave me the same treatment.

I told Kris, "I'd planned on nursing them a year …"

He said, "Well, babies have teeth for a reason. And they eat a lot of food. If they don't want to do it, you can't force them."

That was true. After the difficulty of teaching them, their mastery of it, they'd moved on to something better.

After I stopped nursing them, I started feeding them milk in bottles instead of formula. They immediately began sleeping through the night. I don't know if the formula bothered them, or if they were just at the age that they start sleeping 12 hours consistently. I probably should have done a control and variable experiment between them to test.

Another point made in books was that breastfeeding is all about supply and demand. If they demand it, you'll supply it. I didn't find this to be the case. For instance, when you first have your baby, many women need to place nursing pads in their bras so their breasts don't leak milk. I never once needed one of those, because there was never any extra to go around. Women talk about hearing a baby cry, which makes their milk let down. I didn't have this experience either. My milk would only let down with the assistance of a feeding baby, and even then near the end I would have to visualize rushing waterfalls. (Yes. I would have to concentrate to make myself release milk. Not as instinctive as you would think, is it?!)

Do I ever wonder why I nursed them exclusively those first six weeks of little sleep? Why I didn't just let someone give them a bottle? Yes. Did it even occur to me then? No. I'd decided I was nursing them and I went for it.

Nursing is hard, but human milk is what's best for babies. Even if you only nurse them a little while, you'll be able to pass on your immunities, and you'll feel good about it forever. People always act amazed that I breastfed twins, but once you try it you'll see – it's not really that difficult once they get the hang of it.

But don't get me wrong. The first time they ate food was a really, really exciting day for my nipples.

4. You will love the father of your children more than ever.

When I was six months pregnant, Kris and I went to our first expectant parent class.

A friendly girl, wearing a nametag that said 'Zsh Zsh', said, "What are you having?"

"Twins," I responded.

"I *told* you!" said her husband.

"I was wondering, too," an overweight girl said. "I didn't show until my 27th week."

I bit my tongue.

We were instructed to put our names and due dates on our nametags. I was due way later than any of the other girls, but was way bigger.

The nurse, Arden, started by pointing out that our nametags were circles. "They're ten centimeters in diameter, which is the same size your cervix will need to be before you can push out the baby's head!"

"Her nametag is square," I whispered to Kris. "What does hers mean?"

We giggled like naughty kids in class. Even though at age 29, we were clearly the oldest people in there by about a decade. When I pointed that out, we laughed even harder.

We began going through a workbook together, starting with the smoking talk. She explained that while mothers-to-be know we shouldn't smoke, we should also not have the babies around people smoking.

"Well, my parents smoke," a man named Shawn said. His wife added, "When we're over there, are we supposed to ask them to smoke outside their *own* house?"

"That's something you should start talking about now," Arden counseled. I liked the diplomacy of her answer. A sort of, 'You can't tell people what to do in their own house, but BY GOD think of your child's charred lungs."

We covered pre-term labor, where she asked me to describe Braxton Hicks to everyone, how fathers feel, birth plans, nutrition … basically a lot of stuff Kris and I already knew, since I'd been reading it since I got pregnant.

One of the brochures from the March of Dimes started with this headline, "Even if you do everything right, you can still go into pre-term labor."

"That's the worst headline I've ever seen." I whispered. I had an intense fear of pre-term labor. Like a gentleman, Kris hid the headline with his hand.

As we read through the book, we saw that it was used, and someone else had completed quizzes in it and highlighted certain areas. We made fun of this previous person, and the book, as we listened to the lecturing and conversation around us.

Things we learned:

Tanya: "I have this round ligament pain that starts here," (Gesturing to groin) "and it travels down to my pelvic region, and it basically feels like someone's pulling on my hair."

I could look at no one.

Tasha, whose husband threw away her cigarettes during the smoking talk: "With my first son, I went into pre-labor three times. I had a kidney infection, too."

When we were told how babies in the hospital have bracelets on that set off an alarm when they leave the area …

John Paul, shaking his head: "My dad is 63 and he says sometimes it's better the old way."

Arden replied, "Yes, sometimes the old is good, but the new is even better."

Especially if it reduces the likelihood of your baby being stolen.

Then after the repetition of material I'd been reading about for months, it was exercise time! We all – men and women – got on the floor and did stretches to get us ready for the birth. I could barely do any of them, I was having pretty intense Braxton Hicks, and the effort was making me sweat. It was a real struggle. Arden noted my discomfort and excused me from doing them.

"I'm too big to do any of these!" I whispered to Kris.

Kris laughed, "It seems like they should have another class just for twin moms where they say, 'Don't bother with any of this, since we're just going to cut them out of you anyway.'"

Afterward, we debated whether or not to go back. Did I need to go to a class to learn how to breathe during labor? To tell me not to smoke?

While thinking about this, I asked Kris, "Do you know how to diaper? Or how to bathe a baby?"

"No, but I'd rather learn from you," he said.

"What did you learn in class that you didn't already know?" I asked.

"Um . . . nothing. The relaxation exercise was the best part," he said. "My biggest question during the class was …"

"Yeah?"

"How many of them got married BECAUSE she's pregnant?"

&&&&

So, Kris and I were eager to meet our long-awaited babies. We felt ready, happy, and excited to add to our family.

Books and people emphasize that when you have babies, your world is utterly consumed by them and you forget about the father of your children. They counsel you that you need to force yourself to make time for him, so that he doesn't feel abandoned and shut out.

I experienced the opposite. I was suddenly, irrationally, more concerned about him than ever.

In the first week home, it could have been due to my hormones or the oral steroid prescribed for my PUPPPs rash. (I'd like to blame the medication, obviously.)

Here are a few excerpts about Kris from my journal, starting the day after the babies were born. See if you sense a change …

June 23 - Kris is wonderful.

June 24 – He's a great dad and husband.

June 27 - Kris loves his boys.

June 30 - Kris is always mad at me. Feel strangely disconnected from him. Feel unattractive.

July 1 - I feel a little better, but Kris is mad at me a lot still.

July 4 - Still feel disconnected. Why is he mad??

July 5 - Cried to Kris about him not loving me.

July 12 - Feel normal and don't cry all the time and not worried about Kris loving me.

My mind wasn't completely right, I knew. For instance, one of the first nights we were home I remember distinctly thinking that Cole was mad at me. I told myself that was insane. He was a baby - he just wanted to be fed and held and he wasn't mad. But, since he was a screaming, crying baby looking right at me, he looked accusatory. I forced the thought out of my mind.

I knew about postpartum depression. I didn't have the other symptoms, like fearing I'd hurt my babies. I just became overly concerned about Kris' feelings.

By mid-July when I felt normal, Kris would tell me, "You acted crazy. You just kept saying the same things over and over. Mostly about how I didn't love you."

After I felt normal, I didn't feel like it was just the babies and me. Instead, Kris was more an integral part of my life more than ever. We spent more time together, talking and planning and staring at our kids. When we left them that first month – to go see fireworks, to test-drive a car, to take a spin in our new car – it felt like we were on a first date.

Remember seeing that really cheesy poster of a shirtless man holding a baby? How it was supposed to tug at your heartstrings but instead was grossly saccharine?

Seeing the guy you love holding your babies releases those emotions that poster was trying to bring forth.

Suddenly, everything he did was a little cuter. Holding them. Changing diapers. Playing the piano for them. All of it was suddenly even better than when it was just the two of us.

As an added bonus, there was someone you could leave your children with that didn't need any instruction. (You also didn't have to clean the house for him, like you do babysitters and family members!)

When the boys were a month old I left Kris with the boys and bottles of pumped milk. I went out to dinner with my friends. I came home to a happy husband and kids and, of course, I was happier because I'd gone out for a meal.

They hadn't had a bottle yet. It occurred as I planned on leaving that there was a chance they wouldn't take a bottle, as many babies are reluctant to do. I didn't say anything to Kris, figuring if he didn't know there could be a problem, he wouldn't worry about it.

When I got home, I said, "How did they like their bottles?" He said, "They loved them. They sucked them down in minutes."

Awesome.

A month later I was on my way home from an appointment. Kris called me, frantic.

"They won't stop crying!" I could hear them wailing in the background.

"Are they hungry? They're probably just hungry," I said, full of anxiety. "Just give them a bottle." It was 30 minutes before they normally ate.

I rushed home. By the time I got there, they'd eaten and were happy.

"I don't know why I called you," Kris said. "I knew they were hungry, even though it was early. But when both of them are crying sometimes it's hard to think."

"I know!" I said, happy to have someone who felt the same way as I did.

In all the hundreds of times I've left them, he's never called again. That in itself is cheesy poster-worthy.

&&&&

The father of your child is required to listen to every detail about your children.

When I was pregnant, I was talking to a good friend talk about her baby. I loved my friend and her baby, but I noticed she could really go on.

I forced myself to try and remember this point while I was pregnant, because I knew it wouldn't stick after the babies were born. I thought, "No one cares about your babies as much as you do."

A happy exception from this rule is the father.

Not only does he want to hear about the kids, he wants to talk about them, too. If you want to talk about their looks, personalities, bowel movements – he is required to at least feign interest in everything you say because you're talking about something that's 50% his.

It's freeing. My friends like me, but they don't want to hear about the way my son makes noises while he sleeps. Not for more than a minute anyway. But you throw the father into the mix and bam – not only will he listen, but he'll imitate the sounds with you.

&&&&

I'm not saying that Kris didn't ever hand me a baby and say, "Your son Cole won't stop crying." Or that I've gone to him and said, "I can't do it anymore. I'm going running. Your turn." Or we've put up a light fixture in our living room while my arms are shaking because it's heavy and both boys are crying on the floor and you force yourself to shut it all out so you can mount the fixture because IT NEEDS TO BE DONE, WE BOUGHT THIS LIGHT FIXTURE TWO MONTHS AGO.

What I am saying is that when the babies were born, my world didn't shrink down to just us. It expanded to include all of us together. Our own family.

And if you have twins, especially, it's really helpful to have someone else to carry one of them. Preferably the heavier one.

5. No matter what you do, sometimes babies just cry. If you're used to the idea going in, you'll feel much better when it happens.

When the babies were two weeks old, Kris' sister Meghan stayed the night at our house.

"I'll sleep down here with you and the boys on the couch," she said.

"That's fine …" I said. "I just want you to understand that they cry all night."

"Well, I'm leaving tomorrow, so that means I can take a nap tomorrow afternoon. You can't."

I wasn't going to turn down that offer. So that night was unlike the rest of my nights. When they cried that night between nursings, I would just wake up, look at Meghan, and ask her if she was okay. She always said she was, and I would go back to sleep.

I was later so glad that she was there for verification. So that for the rest of my life I could turn to her and say, "Remember that night you stayed when the babies cried the entire night, no matter what you did to try and make them stop?" And she remembered.

That was one of many, many nights. The rest of them I spent alone. So it was great to have the outsider corroboration.

Some babies cry, some babies don't. Mine cried.

Before I gave birth, Kris and I watched a DVD called *The Happiest Baby on the Block* that a friend recommended to me. We were quite skeptical.

That is, until the babies were home with us, crying. Then we tried everything we'd ever seen or heard about how to comfort babies.

One of the tips was to shush babies. I remember shushing the babies in their bassinet, calmly saying, "Shhhh, shhhh," as their cries grew louder and louder. Eventually my shush turned to, "Shhhh, shhhh … just shut up! Just shut up already!"

I stopped shushing after that.

We gave them pacifiers. They usually spit it out in anger, but I sort of forced them upon them. I thought they would perhaps grow to love them. I would only use them when they went to sleep. They never loved them, and when I took them away at eight months, they didn't miss them for a minute.

Another tip was swaddling. We swaddled them with special swaddling blankets. I could never bring myself to put both arms in, however, since I was trying to encourage thumb sucking. (Which neither of them ever did.)

But they just cried.

It wasn't just at night, though it was mostly at night. During the day they cried much less. In the evening, though, Cole would cry for hours. My friend called it her baby's sour hour. I called it his sour hours, plural. Not as good of a rhyme, but far more accurate.

We tried everything. We'd take him outside on the porch swing, sing to him, play him music, rock him … when you changed what you were doing he'd stop crying for about 30 seconds, then start again.

After a few evenings of that – and what husband doesn't like to be greeted coming home from work by a happy baby, a crying baby, and a tired wife? – I was afraid to accept invitations out of the home at night.

Just to see what would happen, we went to a company baseball game. Even though I was fully prepared for him to cry all night, he was completely happy. We went to dinner at my parents' house. He was completely happy. We spent another evening at home. He cried.

So I learned. Cole hated our house. He cried because he was bored. I didn't know until then that infants cried out of boredom.

So Kris and I hatched a new plan. When he got home, he would take care of Ty and I would strap Cole in the front pack and go for a walk.

Cole never slept on our walks. But he never cried. As we neared our house to go back inside, he would get noticeably agitated.

We weren't going to move to a newer, more interesting house. We weren't going to be gone every night. But the walking helped ease his boredom. And made my ears feel better.

&&&&

Parents whose babies don't cry can't understand this. Sometimes, no matter what you do, they're going to cry. They cried themselves to sleep. They cried when they were hungry, tired, happy, bored, thinking, etc.

I'd also read a lot of books about training your babies to sleep. I was all over it, because I knew there was no chance I was going to be holding two babies and putting them to sleep every time they were tired.

After I moved them upstairs when they were a month old, I moved them into my room. They sometimes preferred sleeping in a bouncy chair or a swing, so I moved those two items, plus a bassinet next to the bed I shared with Kris.

This was a horrible idea. Now, instead of being a floor away from someone who needed to sleep, we were right next to him. Any time the babies cried I felt like I had to stop them to keep Kris from waking up. It was also dark and I was disoriented. One night I fed the same baby twice in a row and left the sleeping one without a feeding, another night I brought a baby into the bed with me and fed him for several hours, apparently.

This situation wasn't working. After a week of that, I put the babies in their own room down the hall.

This is where the sleep training began.

The first night, we all went to bed at the same time. As they cried, and we laid there awake, Kris said, "Now, what exactly are we training them for?"

"We agreed to this!" I said. "We are training them to put themselves to sleep!"

He covered his head with a pillow and forced himself to sleep.

We wised up after that – we went to bed after they'd gone to sleep.

&&&&

Things could've been far worse. When I took the boys in for their appointment I mentioned that Cole cried for two or three hours in the evenings.

"Every night?" the doctor asked.

"No," I said, and explained his boredom problem.

"That doesn't fit the definition of colic," he said. "My son had colic. It was horrible. He cried for three hours, every night for 6 weeks."

See, it could have been worse.

The best things about babies is the older they get, the better they get. Colic doesn't last. Boredom is also eventually alleviated by sitting and moving.

However, you will always see the people with babies that are perfect and never cry. I was lucky enough that my sister had one of each. Her first baby always cried. Her second baby was a happy one and rarely cried. She didn't do anything different.

I experienced this too, but at the same time. One of the best things about having two babies at once is that it makes you feel like you can do no wrong.

For instance, Cole slept through the night long before Ty did. I was treating them and feeding them exactly the same, yet Cole slept and Ty didn't. They reacted differently to the same exact thing. I was absolved!

When the boys were eating the exact same foods, one got constipated, and one didn't. The same food, the same amount – different bowel systems. Absolved!

Cole always loved a room full of people – specifically loud people. Ty always cried when we entered a party. Once again, absolution! I couldn't control their sleeping, their intestines, or their personalities. I never wondered if I was doing the right things the right way. It's a wonderful way to start out parenthood – by realizing that nature beats nurture almost every time.

Don't get me wrong – there are parents who have many babies in a row that never cry. And they think that they're responsible. In a way, they are – their genes have come together to create happy babies. And good for them! My brother and his wife, for instance, had three completely happy babies. Once when I was visiting them and my babies were screaming, they were genuinely perplexed.

"Why are they crying?" my brother asked, amazed at their rage.

"Some babies just cry," I said, hurriedly mixing up bottles.

When they started drinking, they quieted down.

"Oh, they were just hungry," Gage said.

"Gage. They ate an hour ago. They weren't just hungry. They just like to cry. They're eating because I gave them a bottle, and they never turn down food."

When I stopped feeding them and they continued crying, I was a little bit happy they were showing their true colors to others.

That night, the three of us slept in their spare bedroom and the babies cried through the night, as per usual. Since their walls weren't several bricks thick, of course they heard them. I knew they were glad they had happy babies, and I was honestly happy for them.

But for those of us who don't – heed this tip. If you go into it just knowing that they're going to cry, it's a lot easier to deal with when they do.

My mom told me that my sister, my brother, and I were all horrible babies and we cried all the time and only wanted to be held and rocked and didn't want to go to anyone else. So that was my baby experience. I remember holding two babies and looking longingly at the various swings and bouncy chairs they hated and wishing I just had a model of a warm human torso that would hold a baby so I could just *get something done.* Of course, if one of my babies preferred a piece of plastic to hold him over me, I'd probably be jealous. Which is why they must not manufacture those. Right?! Right?!

Even though they cried, my babies liked me more than anyone else – of course, I fed them. But when they cried, people would hand them to me. That had never happened before in my life. I was always the one handing the crying baby away … who wants to hold a crying baby? The mom, that's who. I reverted right back to this after my babies weren't babies anymore. I hand crying babies back to the mothers because I know that's where they want to be.

My babies are toddlers now and they still cry sometimes and they still love me to hold them. It's just who they are. And as the days are fleeting that they want to be held, I hold on to them a little longer, I squeeze them a little tighter, I kiss them a little more. One of the most beautiful parts of having babies is that it's ephemeral. The first time the babies cried in unison in my ears I thought it was the most musical sound I'd ever heard, at the same time knowing it would drive me crazy in just a few short weeks.

So, know that they're going to cry. Understand that it's okay if they do. And look forward to the day when they can finally answer you when you plead, "Just *tell* me what's wrong!"

6. Twins will wake each other up.

While I was pregnant, a friend gave me *On Becoming Babywise*, by Gary Ezzo & Robert Bucknam. I really liked the book (I still do,) and I took great comfort in particular section that read: "If your multiple babies have been sharing a room since birth, they won't wake each other up. They will learn to shut out each other's crying, so don't separate them when one is fussing."

Though my babies went through a forced separation in the hospital, the first night we were home they started sleeping together. I thought they would find comfort from another body in the bed – after all, they'd just spent months sharing the same space. (One might say fighting over the same space, but hey.)

They slept in a bassinet together. Cole seemed happiest with his nose smashed into Ty's back.

When they first woke each other up with their crying, I guessed it was because they had five days apart in the hospital. I thought it wasn't too late for them to learn to tolerate each other. I kept it up.

At a month old, they moved from the bassinet to a crib in their room. They were still waking each other up. I imagine it's difficult to ignore someone screaming in your ear.

By the time they were three months old, I knew it was time to separate them. I'd enter their room at night to feed them, and there would be Ty, screaming and head-butting Cole as hard as he could. There was Cole, trying to sleep and finally being awakened by someone smashing into his head. It just looked too mean – who could possibly sleep like that? After I separated them into their own rooms and cribs, they each slept more soundly.

However, their cries still woke each other up.

My first attempt at white noise came as a pleasant mistake. I used an old fan my parents gave me in the hallway to circulate air because it was warm in our upstairs. They slept so soundly – I was amazed at how effective it was. Not only did I not wake up at every little snort and snuffle, but they didn't wake each other up.

As I got closer to their rooms I realized … oh. They were crying. Both of them. The old fan was just so loud that it blocked out all noise.

While it was tempting to continue using it, I decided there was a definite downside to not being able to hear anything at all. I purchased a $10 box fan at Wal-Mart and decided to try it out.

It worked well for them and me. Again, since I was so in tune to their cries, I could now sleep through a cough and would only wake up if they cried. And since they were now separated by a fan and a hallway, they didn't wake each other up.

This continued to work throughout their babyhood and into toddlerhood. When they became loud two-year-olds who woke up in the morning, stood up, and began yelling, "MOMMY! COME GET ME!" at the top of their lungs, there's no chance a little fan is going to protect one's ears from that sound.

I visited a friend with infant twins and two older children. She put them to bed – all on the same floor, with the twins sharing a room – and then we were able to converse normally in the living room. It was all very close quarters and I admired how she'd taught her children to sleep through normal sounds.

A month later she emailed me and said that her twins were teething and crying and waking each other up. She said she wished she had another room so she could separate them. She wrote, "We've tried letting them cry, but it's so much easier to deal with one at a time - though it's constant throughout the night with bits and pieces of sleep . . . if they cry, they inevitably wake the other up and then we have two screaming babies . . . each night as I'm frustrated I try to keep telling myself this is the last time I have to do this, it might be hell now, but in the end it will be done one day! Please tell me this is so and that it is sooner rather than later!?"

While I felt sorry for her, I was certainly glad I wasn't the only one with twins who woke each other up. And I'm certain we weren't the only two mothers. It just makes sense. As adults, we like it dark and quiet when we sleep. As babies, you don't want someone you have to be around ALL THE TIME screaming right next to you.

If you don't have enough bedrooms, maybe try putting a crib an office, a walk-in closet, or even a bathroom. (These are all places my kids have slept at other people's houses. Because it's difficult to limit our overnight visits with friends to people who can only offer three extra bedrooms.)

&&&&

I often tell people that the first six weeks of their lives were a blur, but after that it was fun.

That was for a variety of factors (see painful rash, surgery recovery), but there were two main ones -

Factor one: lack of sleep. Thankfully, I've never needed a lot of sleep. Many nights I'd add up the hours I got (all interrupted with feeding and comforting), and it would equal four, five, or six. I considered anything six and above to be a success, but even four was manageable. It's not like lack of sleep kept us from doing anything – we had reunions, church camp, hosted a pool party, had friends stay over – you just do it less well-rested. I did some test experiments to see if caffeine affected the babies at all. It didn't seem to ever do anything to them. After I discerned that, I would have a diet pop in the morning right after I nursed them, to make sure it was out of my system three hours later.

Factor two: learning about my new life. When I was pregnant with twins, people would say things like, "I could barely manage with one baby – I can't imagine having two!" Let's be straight here. Aside from reading and babysitting, I knew very little about babies. I knew in theory what it was like, but I didn't know what it was like in reality.

One moment particularly stands out. It was my second day home with the babies. I'd just gotten up, fed them, changed them, clothed them, and put them to sleep. I went to the kitchen during my two and a half hour break to make myself some toast. I got out the peanut butter jar, which was almost empty. I scraped a little of it out and then *threw the container away*. The pre-baby Carla would have put it back into the cupboard and spent a good 60 seconds next time scraping out the very last bits of it, until I was only getting peanut butter molecules. The post-baby Carla didn't have time to deal with that. TIME WAS A WASTIN'. As I regarded it in the trash, I thought, *This is my life now.* The unimportant things were going to fall by the wayside for awhile.

&&&&

Unless you live in a house with two wings and soundproof doors, some twins will wake each other up. I'm all for co-sleeping twins – you have to wake them both up to feed them anyway. But I also think there's a point where they are like any other person … they need peace and quiet. So get a cheap fan, shut the doors, and get a good night's sleep.

7. No matter how painful it seems, sleep training with twins is worth it.

Before I had my own kids, when I heard of people with their babies on 'a schedule', I didn't quite get it. It seemed to me that their entire day was organized around being home when the baby was sleeping. If they had other plans, why wouldn't the baby just sleep in a car seat, or skip a nap?

The books talked about attachment parenting, which has more of an emphasis on the baby, instead of the clock. Mothers of twins told me no - I'd definitely want them on a schedule.

In the beginning, it's easy. Newborns sleep a lot during the day. Sometimes they'd only be awake for ten minutes after nursing them before they'd fall asleep again. Over time, they would take actual naps. For instance, mine took three a day for ages. Then they eventually dropped their late evening nap and took only two naps. When they were age two, they stopped taking two naps and started taking one.

After awhile, I completely understood why people put their babies on a schedule. It's for this reason – kids are really awful if they don't sleep. My children have never drifted off to sleep on the floor or a lawn or a lap. They get crazier and more irritable and rowdy the more tired they get – they eventually will do anything to try and stay awake. They get wild.

Thus, the naps and the bedtime.

If you only have one baby, I'm sure it's much easier to put him to sleep. When you have two, they need to learn how to put themselves to sleep.

From the beginning, I didn't let the babies fall asleep in my arms. I'd hold them, kiss them, put them down, then walk away. Since I started doing it from birth, it wasn't like there was a whole breaking of habit – they were just always used to it.

A friend of mine with twins told me when I was pregnant, "You have to sleep train. It makes your life and their lives easier forever. My seven-year-olds tell me when they're tired and go right to bed. It's great."

At two, my kids started telling me this too. We'd be reading to them at night before bed and they'd say, "I want to go to bed."

It was music to my ears.

It wasn't easy in the beginning. You want to cradle a baby. You want him to fall asleep on you, so soft and sweet. But the crying that comes when you set him down … hardly worth it. Or lying in bed in a cold sweat there when they're six months old, wondering when they're going to stop crying.

Also, after the babies stopped eating during the night (nine months) we never went in their rooms for anything. They never wake up, and they apparently love to sleep. It's not like a punishment for them – they are entirely ready to take a nap and go to bed. The boys know when they're going to bed – they expect it – and they enjoy the schedule.

Yes, I organize my day around my kids. If I didn't, I'd be dragging crabby, sleep-deprived kids around. And no one would want to be anywhere near us.

&&&&

Don't get me wrong … I wanted my kids to sleep more than anything. I gave them pacifiers. I would nurse them in the night. I would do anything to get them to sleep, except hold them as they drifted off.

Then, when my babies were a month old, a terrible tragedy occurred. My cousin's baby died of SIDS.

Since people have been placing their babies on their stomachs to sleep, giving them blankets, and sleeping with them since the beginning of time - with no ill effects - many people disregard SIDS warnings. I understand this. When you're a parent you will do anything to make your baby happy, so if he seems happier on his stomach, of course you want him to sleep that way.

However, I took the warnings seriously. I placed my babies on their backs and didn't even give them a blanket until they were one year old. (I dressed them in layers. And kept the house warm.)

Therefore, their little beds didn't look so comfortable. I'd place my babies in their stark, empty cribs and whisper, "Enjoy your cage," as I left the room.

Some nights this didn't work. I'd think about how they liked their car seats … and a few nights I'd place them in their car seats next to their cribs and they'd sleep in those.

They liked it because their car seats were cuddling them, holding them tighter than they felt in the bed. (Even tighter than their swaddling could be.) I liked it, because I knew that if they were strapped in a car seat, they were upright and fine.

But I wanted them to learn to sleep in beds – I thought that I was restricting their movement. I thought about how uncomfortable I would be sleeping in a car seat. Or even sitting in one for an extended period of time. And adult car seats are actually cushioned – not a piece of cloth over plastic like most of the infant car seats today. So I kept putting them back in their beds until they eventually preferred it. Once they could roll over on their own, they slept on their stomachs for the rest of their babyhood.

So – schedules, lying them down when they're still awake, and using a car seat if you need to. The only bed with true safety features.

&&&&

There was a lot more I didn't understand before I had kids. A friend told me, "You better get a big bed, because all your kids are going to be in there with you." I laughed, thinking there was no way one of my kids would sleep in my bed. (This, despite my recollection of creeping into my parents' bed and trying to stay as far as I could on the edge so my mom wouldn't notice me and make me go back to my bed. She tells me I stopped doing this when I was about seven.) And again, it's so tempting. The problem with kids is that once you do something, it sets a precedent. I feel like there can't be a one-off incident, because they remember and learn and expect certain outcomes from certain behaviors. So I felt if I took them in our bed even once, then they would look forward to it and want to be in our bed.

I also wondered why people would go to crying babies when the babies were obviously just tired. Why didn't they just let them cry? We'd heard of people dealing with 'crying it out' and how hard it was, and been with friends who went into the baby's room about a million times, cradling him and rocking him until he finally went to sleep hours later.

This is what I learned: one will do anything to sleep and have your babies sleep. Anything. It just makes everyone so much happier to have a good night's rest. It's not like kids have some coffee in the morning and can suck it up. They are actively unhappy when they don't have enough sleep. And the parents – of course – once you can't sleep every second you think you might want to (which is what the situation was for many people before having kids) it becomes precious.

So the sooner a baby can go to sleep and stay asleep by himself, the more sleep you can all have. Though it may seem cruel to not hold a baby as he drifts off, you'll feel much better about it when all of you are getting adequate sleep.

8. Depend on yourself.

Over and over while I was pregnant I read this advice: If people offer to help, take them up on it. I thought it was great advice – people wouldn't offer if they didn't want to help. But what that doesn't take into account is how accomplished you feel when you can do something yourself.

The day I brought Cole home from the hospital my in-laws were coming over to meet the babies for the first time – and my house was a disaster. I didn't have the time or energy to clean it, and Kris was out delivering calves.

My mom came over and cleaned up and even vacuumed my house as I sat nursing them on the couch, crying. I felt so helpless and useless. She'd already done a lot for me – come to the hospital with me, driven me, held Ty while I was with Cole in the NICU – and here I was reduced to watching her clean my house. It was a low moment.

Shouldn't I have been thrilled that she volunteered to clean for me? Happy that someone was doing work that I flat-out didn't have time to do? Thinking I deserved that kind of treatment after the long week I'd had?

I wasn't. I was really glad my house wasn't going to be a sty while my in-laws visited, but I was embarrassed I was incapable.

A few weeks later, still feeling like I didn't want to use the time I had to clean, I hired a housecleaner. She was a lovely woman who did a great job at a fair price and I loved coming home to a clean house. The downside – I felt guilty for hiring someone to do something I was completely capable of doing – just that I couldn't do it all at once. Also, since I was paying someone to clean, there wasn't much in between cleaning that I performed. Third, I hated having to leave the house for three hours on a certain day during certain hours. Not that I wasn't out and about a lot – but I didn't like coming home, realizing she was still there, and driving around the block until she left.

Worst of all, I was a tad ashamed. I cleaned my grandma's and my great aunt's houses every week from age 12-18. It wasn't like I didn't know how to clean. I realized that I really liked to talk about it with other people who had housecleaners so that they could continue to list the reasons why it made sense.

After awhile, it became more of a bother to have a housecleaner than to not have one. Plus, there was the whole saving money issue.

I felt like it was a challenge. Could I keep the house as clean as a housecleaner?

No, not really. My house is never all really clean all at the same time. Unless company's coming over.

But it's *cleaner* all of the time. It's not an every-two-weeks thing, it's a daily thing. Just a little here and there when it needs it.

Whether your housecleaner is volunteer or paid, there's an immense sense of satisfaction that comes from being able to do something yourself. Oddly, sometimes that even includes cleaning toilets.

&&&&

One of the most amazing things that happened when I had the babies is that our neighbors brought food over. Most of them were my parents' friends and my church community when I grew up.

I vowed then and there that I was going to take food over to people's houses when they had a baby, because I have never been so hungry or grateful.

Chicken potpie. Cookie ice cream sandwiches. Chicken and rice. Caramel desserts. Cinnamon rolls and homemade jam. It didn't matter that I didn't normally eat these things. It didn't matter that I didn't normally eat meat. They were barely back in their cars before I was shoving it into my mouth.

A friend of mine belonged to a church where people signed up to bring dinners to the new family for two weeks. She always signed up, and when she became pregnant, she hoped that she'd make the list. They failed to add her, and she didn't get any church dinners. The fact that she then changed churches was probably a coincidence, but it is useful to prove a point – no matter how satisfactory it can be to be able to have a baby or babies and whip up a healthy, hearty meal – there's no substitute for someone placing a hot meal into your hands.

When my babies were a few months old, I decided to return the favor. (The time before that when I re-gifted one of my frozen lasagnas for another person's baby didn't count.) I was bound and determined to help another family out.

Church friends down the road had a newborn. I called and asked which day they'd like me to bring dinner. She gave me a day and a time.

I decided to make them one of my standards – calzones. While the babies were taking a nap I prepared the dough, chopped the peppers and tomatoes and thawed the spinach. I put everything into containers and transported it, as well as the babies in their car seats, down the road to the neighbors' house. I made several trips inside, carrying babies, a cookie sheet with the dough on it, the ingredients, etc.

She was in another room nursing the baby. She yelled to me that she was having trouble with the baby's eating that day, and that she'd try and come in when she was done. Her older daughter wandered in and out of the room, afraid of me.

My babies sat in their car seats and Ty began to cry. I could hear her baby crying in the other room. I rocked Ty with my foot as I tried to put together the food. I had imagined the two of us in the kitchen, chatting away as we worked, talking as they baked the 20 minutes and eating it together. Once I was there, it was obvious it was not going to work that way – and that I was not going to be joining her for dinner and my idea of what was going to happen was, in a word, wrong.

I threw the calzones together, scribbled 350 for 20 minutes on a piece of paper, and skedaddled out of there … to a home with no dinner for me or Kris.

Perhaps I wasn't ready for the giving-meals step.

You can use your experience as a benchmark. The day you have babies, can give another family dinner, and have your own too – you're officially past the hard point of twins.

Or even better, if someone you know is having a baby now, before you give birth, take them a meal. Depending on how much you give, you might get quite the payoff afterward!

&&&&

The first time I took the babies to the doctor's office was when they were eight days old. I purposely scheduled it at a time and day when I knew my mom would be able to go with me. I didn't feel that I'd be able to do it all by myself.

I started preparing to go to the doctor's office as soon as I woke up in the morning. I was timing their feedings, my shower, the drive time …. My mom came over five minutes before I had to leave and we loaded the boys and my diaper bag in the car.

I was frantic that we were going to be late. My mom, calmly in the passenger seat, said, "It's going to be fine … we're not going to be late … just concentrate on your driving."

We arrived at the exact time of our appointment. My mom helped me carry them in, undress them to be weighed, calm them afterward, re-diaper them, sit through the appointment, carry them out, and transport them into the house. I was exhausted.

A week later, my mom went with me to the second appointment too. It just made it easier.

By the time they were a month old, I made an appointment when I knew my mom was working. I took them lots of other places by myself – the grocery store, for instance – and I figured that I was perfectly capable of doing this.

The people in the doctor's office stared when I came in carrying a car seat in each hand. There were a lot of questions and compliments on their cuteness which I lapped up on their behalf.

I felt accomplished – the nurses, the doctors, the staff – they all saw and knew that I was able to take care of my children *all by myself*. Best of all, I knew it myself.

&&&&

Of course, everything is easier when they can't move.

Like I said, when I first took the babies in for their checkup at one month, the nurses came flocking in droves from the other rooms to come and see the tiny babies and coo and ooh and ahh and pronounce them beautiful and perfect and tell me to enjoy it because they're going to grow up so fast. They would exclaim gaily over their weights and expressions and little faces. The children inevitably peed when they were un-diapered and put on the scale.

No one seemed to mind.

When they got older and I carried them in, one car seat in each hand, the comments shifted a little. Though they would still admire them, they began to say things like, "I don't know how you do it!"

Once the boys walked in there under their own power, it was a whole different experience for everyone.

At their 15-month appointment, I herded the boys into the examination room.

"Hello!" the nurse said. "You're Carla, right?"

"Yes," I said. "Have you been our nurse before? I'm afraid I don't remember your name."

"Yes! I'm Stephanie. I was your nurse for their one-month visit, and I went home and told my husband ALL about this mom with twins that came in and how I just didn't know HOW she did it. I told him I hope we never have twins! I really enjoy napping!" she said cheerfully.

I wasn't sure how to respond. I hope you don't have twins either?

"How is it with them?" she asked, eyeing them knowingly.

"Great!" I said, trying not to be defensive. "We have a lot of fun." As I was saying this, both boys sat on my lap, clinging to me, being terrified of her.

"Do you stay home with them?" she asked.

"Yeah," I answered, trying to peel one boy off of me to start the unclothing for the appointment.

"That must be nice," she said, obviously testing me to make sure I didn't start raving about how I couldn't wait to get out of the house. I didn't fall for her little ploy.

I stripped them down to their diapers. She weighed them, measured them, and left us in the room as we waited for the doctor.

Unfortunately, the room was not meant for toddlers. Cole opened the cupboard doors and began rummaging around in the sample drugs. Ty headed straight for the electrical outlet, which the examination table was plugged into. Above the outlet, a little bit of the plaster was coming off. Ty stuck his finger right in and began to help by chipping it away. Cole finished looking through the drugs and began to push buttons on the table, moving it up and down. I tried to prevent them from causing any serious damage, but still allowed them to have a good time. It wasn't my fault the room wasn't baby-proofed.

After the doctor's examination, two nurses returned to give the boys shots. Again Stephanie, and an older nurse named Bernie.

"I don't know how you do it!" Stephanie repeated.

"I have two children – ages 7 and 9 – but I had them two years apart!" Bernie said.

"Oh, you know," I said, "by now it's just like having two kids." Bernie gave me a plastic smile, which seemed to mean that she thought I was lying.

The nurses held them down and gave them shots. As soon as they stood them up, the boys reached down and simultaneously ripped off four band aids, causing blood to stream down their four legs.

"Oh! My!" Stephanie said, reaching for a paper towel.

"I'll get it," I said, knowing that they wouldn't want to wipe up someone's blood without gloves. She handed me the paper towel, and I blotted at their legs. They watched me, apparently surprised by the entire turn of events. Had no children torn off their band aids before? Or just not everyone in unison? Bernie put two more band aids on Ty and I wrestled him into his pants before he could take them off. Cole had stopped bleeding, so I didn't bother with the band aids.

I picked both of them up and readied to head out the door.

"Wow!" Stephanie said. "I can't believe you can carry them both at one time!"

I never remember that people find this unusual. Since they grow so slowly, it's easy to pick them up at the same time … because I'm in an amazing, years-long weight lifting program.

I walked to the checkout desk and put Cole down. He immediately ran away, into the hallway. While still holding Ty, I followed him, trying to get him to leave with me. He raced into a room where there were three nurses perched on stools.

"Oh, he's adorable! Wow, I bet you have your hands full. My, isn't he energetic!" Their words overlapped each other. With Ty under one arm, I scooped Cole up with my free arm, setting the nurses off again.

Bernie and Stephanie waved goodbye. I knew they were going to go and talk about us.

I knew that I was serving as birth control for the entire office.

When I returned for their 18-month appointment, we had yet another new nurse. Michelle was friendly, talked right to the boys, got down on their level, showed genuine interest … and they thought she was terrifying. Whenever she got near them, they'd cling to me and cry. She was pulling out stickers, pictures of her own kids - anything to get them on her side. They were having none of it.

"Can you stand against the wall so I can measure you?" she asked Cole.

"No! No!" he screamed, twisting away from her and reaching for me.

"How about you, Ty? Can I measure you?" she asked.

"NOOOOOO!" Ty cried, hanging around my neck.

"We'll just put them on the scale then," she said.

She picked up Cole and he reached out for me as if he were being abducted, screaming, tears streaming down his face.

"It's just right over here!" she said, sounding like she was trying not to panic.

She put Cole on the scale. He saw the buttons on the side and began pushing them repeatedly, making the scale readout not work. She tried to prevent him from pushing the buttons, which set him off crying again and trying to escape. Repeat for Ty.

Back in the room, she had to lie them down on the paper-covered table to get their heights. They acted as if she was burning them.

I put both of them on my lap to calm them after she was done.

"Wow, your mom must be a superwoman!" she said as she left the room.

Translated: "Your children are holy terrors and it's a wonder you haven't abandoned them!"

Dr. Gold came in – they like him and were angels while he was there. He said, "This is the easiest examination of 18-month old twins I've ever had!"

Since he'd heard them screaming in the halls, he had obviously been expecting far worse. Set the bar low!

Michelle returned with a pregnant nurse, named Karen.

"She's going to have a little boy just like you!" Michelle said to my kids.

"Did you just find out?" I asked Karen.

"Well," Karen said, patting her stomach, "since I work here, I found out really early. And then I just kept hoping the boy part was going to fade away … but it never did."

"Ha ha!" I forced, watching them get ready to give my male children really painful shots.

There obviously must be a reason she doesn't want a boy – maybe she already has a houseful of girls. "Do you have other children?"

"No," she said, sighing. "This is our first."

I looked at my boys. They were in their diapers, barefoot, happy, both pulling the stirrups in and out of the examination table. How could she not want a little boy? How bad were boys that she didn't even want to give birth to one?

We laid Ty down to get his shots and he screamed because he knew what was coming.

Cole didn't cry even when he got the shots.

Cole wouldn't allow them to apply band aids – he batted away their hands as they tried to stick them on.

"Wow," Michelle told him, "you're tough!"

The pregnant nurse looked weary.

I picked up my kids, one on each hip, and said, "Yep, they're tough as nails. Good luck with the rest of your pregnancy!"

"Thanks - I don't know how you do it – twins!" she said.

I ignored the stares of the nurses and people in the waiting room as I carried them out. I thought about it as I drove home - and I got it. Nurses see kids at their absolute worst. They see sick kids, kids who don't want to be poked or prodded – never kids at their best. They probably dread seeing them. And multiply that by two.

Come to think of it, I've never had the same nurse two times in a row. Either they have a lot of nurses working there, or they rotate our visits so everyone can experience a brief moment of what it's like to have two kids the same age - so they can talk about us later.

I can just imagine them gathering in the break room after we leave. One of them says to the others, "I told her she must be … superwoman!" (Chorus of raucous giggles.)

Or … maybe the nurses are there to make me feel good. Anytime people think I'm doing something hard or impressive, I laugh it off, because I'm not doing anything different than anyone else in the history of the world that's raised kids.

Except maybe carrying two kids at one time. That's the best part of the doctor visit – finding out exactly how much weight I'm lugging around. *All by myself.*

9. Even if you think you know everything about birth, it's different when it's you.

When I was single and 24 years old, I had the living room of my dreams. For the first time in my life, I had cable and a treadmill.

I loved flipping through the 80-some channels as I ran, and it so happened that there was a show on when I ran at 10am every day – *Wedding Story*.

Wedding Story is a show that tells the story of a couple – how they met, how he proposed – and then shows their rehearsal, wedding, and reception.

Since I was getting married in four months, I thought it was kind of an instructive show. I took notes on the vows people said. I was very interested in their decorations and programs. But as my wedding date crept nearer, the show took on a nightmarish quality.

"You're supposed to have handmade favors? I'm supposed to buy him a gift? Her hair looks great

– should I do mine like that? Why didn't I get built-in boobs?" I'd yell at my TV.

Eventually, I stopped watching it altogether. It was just too frightening seeing things that I may have missed, or was supposed to do … or find other glaring inadequacies that I was blissfully unaware of before that stupid show came into my life.

So I wouldn't even flip past it on accident, I began running a half hour later and discovered the show *Baby Story*. I saw one child birthed and decided I didn't know which show was scarier.

But, my wedding day came and everything was perfect. The spell *Wedding Story* had on me was broken – now I enjoyed watching it when I ran. And since *Baby Story* came on right afterward, I began watching that, too.

Now, I have seen more births than a first-year gynecologist. I've seen women have sextuplets, quadruplets, conjoined twins, preemies, c-sections, and water births. I've seen them make plaster casts of their stomachs, paint henna on their tummies, and wear those overalls that seem really not-helpful to a woman who has to pee all the time. I've seen them have their first, third, and eighth child.

This show is formulaic too – you're introduced to the family, you hear about how they met and married, and how she told him she was pregnant.

Then they go to the hospital and she has the baby. For the last five minutes, they interview the couple at home a few months later while they hold a quiet, beautiful, sleeping infant.

When I saw the first birth, I was catapulted back into ninth grade biology class, where I thought it was the most horrific and painful and stomach-wrenching sight I'd seen. There was so much liquid and angst. (But the angst might have been coming from the people actually in the room with me.) And most of all, the woman didn't make any sound. It was nothing like the women I'd seen in sitcoms.

But as I watched birth after birth, I realized that no woman really makes much sound. (I'd seen cows give birth before and they didn't make much noise, and they had no drugs at all! But if that cow was in a sitcom …) And what followed after the birth was pretty much the same, too – they plop the baby up on the mom, it's gross, they towel it off and call it good, even though it looks like it could use a good scrubbing, everyone cries, (including some viewers, depending on whether I liked the people or not, sometimes I was a little sad these wackos were bringing another life into the world), and umbilical cords are really hard to cut.

So I got used to it, and it no longer was scary, either. I began to think that someday - someday – this might be something I could handle.

Then, they changed the formula.

The new show now starts at the hospital as the woman has the baby. In between shots, the woman narrates from the future about her experience.

"It felt like someone was ripping my spine out and then reaching in and pulling my guts out, then trying to squish them all in at the same time. I wish I could describe the pain I was in right there. I wanted drugs immediately," a new mom said.

So did I, at that point. Where's the beauty of childbirth?

If that wasn't bad enough, then they set up a camera in the couple's bedroom to capture the baby's first night home.

So you see bedraggled, anxious, sleep-deprived people trying to tend to a tiny infant. Running on the treadmill got very hard at this point.

Then they do some activity, like the mom goes to get a haircut while the dad stays home and takes care of the baby. Expect 5-7 phone calls between the two of them for this section.

I never made it to the end of one of the new shows. Every time I got 20 minutes in, I'd hop off the treadmill to count my birth control pills.

&&&&

So by the time I actually became pregnant, I'd watched a million more births. The night before I went in for my scheduled c-section, I watched a video of a spinal block and c-section on Mayo Clinic's web site.

The needle going into her spine looked long. I was glad I'd watched it so I knew just what was going on. I like to be very informed. I didn't want any surprises along the way.

My doctor had already taken the time to answer every single question that I had. So by the time I went in for surgery, I was feeling prepared.

Kris and I set our alarms and went into the hospital. We had to walk a really long way to get to the actual room. It was the furthest I'd walked in quite awhile. I checked in and went into a room. I changed into a gown and had monitors put on the babies. Kris and I read the newspaper and just hung out for awhile. My doctor had told me that my surgery was scheduled for 10am and that they would be running late, because they always did. It was actually a little bit reassuring when they told me it was going to be later … I liked to know that he could tell the future.

I walked to the operating room, feeling huge and like everyone was looking at me. I reminded myself that this had happened to millions of women millions of times and that this was no big deal at all to anyone except Kris and me.

They took me in the operating room while Kris got his scrubs on. The doctors told me that they didn't like to husbands to see the epidural given because too many of them passed out.

I sat on the operating table and talked to the anesthesiologist. He looked young and had a slight southern accent.

"Have you done hundreds of these?" I asked. I like experience on my side.

"Hundreds," he answered. "Do you understand what's going to happen?"

"Yes … I watched a video of it online last night," I said.

"What?" he said, then recovering, "You mean … you watched a video of someone giving an epidural?"

"Yes, on the Mayo Clinic site," I said.

"Hmm. That must have been interesting. Then you do know what's going to happen," he said, laughing.

"That needle looked really long!" I said. "I don't need to see it!"

"Did you already get your IV?" he asked, referring to the plug they put in my hand in order to easily change out intravenous fluids and medications. It was just a needle inserted into the top of my hand with a rubber plug attached. Then they put tape over it so it wouldn't move around.

"Yes," I answered, waving it at him.

"That hurts way more than this will," he said. (I wondered how he knew. Had he had an epidural? Somehow I doubted it. But I still trusted his honest face.) "Don't worry. Just hunch your back over and stay really still."

I leaned over (as best I could, with a giant stomach in front of me), and he said, "Just a little bee sting," and inserted the needle.

I've been stung by bees at least fifteen times in my life. One time ten times in one day, actually. (Five on each leg during a very memorable family hike! Have you heard of ground bees? They were new to me!) And his description was incredibly apt. It did feel like a bee sting.

I was shivering. I couldn't tell if it was out of nervousness or medication. I asked them and they said, "Everyone shivers."

Kris and the two surgeons came in – my doctor, and his assistant Catalina, whom I'd met that day. They were completely covered. Goggles, hats, gloves, and boots that went up to their knees.

"Wow!" I said. "I understand the goggles and gloves, but what's up with those boots? Are you planning on wading around in a bloodbath?"

They only sort of laughed. Dr. Roth said, "It's as much for our protection as yours." I'm assuming that was his standard answer for any patient invoking the word bloodbath.

They had warned me before that some people became panicky when the numbness reached their lungs because they felt like they were suffocating. It was an unusual sensation, but I didn't feel like I couldn't breathe. I did, however, want to make sure they knew what they were doing.

"Are you sure I'm numb enough?" I asked Dr. Roth. "I can still feel a lot."

"Let's test," he said. He took something sharp and poked me below my collarbone. It was enough to tell it was sharp. He continued poking me in a line down my skin, and when he got about halfway down my torso, I could still feel the pressure, but it didn't hurt. It was the strangest feeling to feel something that you knew should hurt – but didn't.

"How does a spinal block work?" I asked.

"They figured out how to fool your brain into not feeling pain," he said.

"That's so amazing!" I said. "Let's just hope it lasts through the entire operation! I'll let you know," I joked.

They set up the curtain in front of me. They administered medicine through my IV and I immediately felt faint.

"I'm going to pass out!" I alerted the anesthesiologist. "I am NOT going to miss the birth of my babies! Please help!"

"I'm adjusting it right now," he said. I started to feel a little better. Then I didn't.

"I'm going to throw up! Right now!" I told them. They put a bowl near my head.

"I'm still adjusting," he said. "How do you feel now?"

The feeling of fainting and puking subsided and I felt good.

"I'm fine!" I said. "Go ahead with the surgery!"

The doctors and Kris all laughed. I hadn't meant to be funny.

"We … weren't really waiting for you," Dr. Roth said.

I had already told Dr. Roth that I wanted to see my babies being born, so he already planned on taking the curtain away when he pulled them out. But I felt left out at the beginning part of it. So I started asking questions.

"Are they cutting into me now, Kris?"

"Yep."

"Is there a lot of blood?"

"No," Kris said, obviously wondering how descriptive he should be. "They're sort of cauterizing as they go."

"Does it look like the tool you use to dehorn the calves?" I asked.

"Sort of …" he said, fascinated with the operation.

"You can take pictures," Dr. Roth said. "Go ahead."

"Take some! Take some!" I urged.

Kris leaned in to get a closer picture.

"*Not that close*!" the two doctors said in unison as he leaned in too close to my incision. He backed off and got many good photos. I couldn't look at them until my stomach had healed.

"What are you doing now?" I asked.

"Now we're moving the muscles to the side to get to the uterus," Dr. Roth said. I could feel them pulling and tugging my innards.

"Here comes Baby A," he said. A nurse took down the curtain and I watched as he pulled out a baby by his head.

"It's a boy!" he said happily.

"Ty Kristopher!" I said in response.

I watched them grab onto a squirming, gooey leg. He pulled, pulled, pulled out the baby by his leg. I felt an amazing weight lift off my internal organs and felt like I was taking the first deep breath I'd ever taken. I felt so light.

"It's another boy!" Dr. Roth said.

"Cole Anderson!" I said in genuine surprise, since I was certain that one of the babies was going to be a girl.

Nurses whisked the babies to waiting beds in the room. I could see Ty, but Cole was out of my line of sight.

"Are they okay? Is Cole crying? Are they okay?" I kept asking Kris.

"They're fine," he said. "You can see – they're fine," he said.

"I can't see Cole," I said. "Please go over there and see if he's fine." Kris did. In the meantime, I could feel them finishing up with my uterus. I could feel them pushing out the rest of the baby stuff – yes, that's a technical term.

Kris came back to my head to assure me that Cole was crying and breathing adequately and that they were bringing them to me soon.

"Here, Kris, take a picture of this!" Dr. Roth said.

"What's that?" Kris asked, snapping one.

"It's her uterus!" he said happily.

I was excited to see that one. I like now to show that picture to people about to have babies. It looks like the doctor is holding a raw chicken just above my body.

The nurses came over and handed the babies to Kris and me. I held one in each arm as they wheeled me out of the operating room. They both were crying in my ears. It was the sweetest, most beautiful sound I'd ever heard. I'd been waiting so long to hear it. I knew that in a few weeks I would cringe when I heard it, but at that moment I couldn't have been happier.

They push a button in the hallway that plays a little tune to let everyone on the floor know that another baby has been born. They told me to push it twice.

They took us to the recovery room, where we would stay and be monitored for two hours before moving to my hospital room. A nurse sat outside a curtained area, and Kris and I were alone with our babies for the first time.

I was drugged. I was flying high and feeling great. I could not stop scratching my nose. It itched so much. And I had a lot of trouble keeping track of which baby was which baby. The nurse finally slapped nametags on their hats so I was able to keep them straight.

I'd been worried – even though I knew my babies were fraternal, I was skeptical of my ability to tell them apart. After all, before that point, babies pretty much all looked alike to me. But immediately, it was obvious that they didn't look alike.

POINT - I read a twin book that said, "Do not ever admit to anyone – especially your children – that you were unable to tell them apart, even in pictures. Imagine how this would make them feel."

Okay, I must disagree. Twin books give tips on how to tell babies apart – paint one of their toenails a color, put a waterproof bracelet on one, etc. I knew from the beginning that mine didn't look alike. And yet, when I look at pictures of them when they were babies, they look alike. If I have both of them in a picture, I can compare them and discern who is who. But you know why it's difficult to tell one by himself? BECAUSE BABIES LOOK ALIKE. They look like babies. Go ahead and tell your kids. They won't be damaged by this assertion. And if they are, then they're going to need thicker skin to make it in this harsh world.

When the babies were in the womb, they'd been labeled Baby A and Baby B. We'd assigned names to them based on the letters. Baby A was going to be Ty Kristopher, with his middle name after his father. Baby B was going to be Cole Anderson, Anderson being my maiden name. While we were in the recovery room, Kris and I studied every part of them. We immediately agreed that Cole looked exactly like a Wardin.

Kris held Cole, looked at me, and looked at the nurse. He whispered, "It's not too late to switch their names."

"We are not switching their names!" I said. Though it was true it would be nice to have their looks in line with their namesakes, I kind of liked the idea of blending our family's names and traits.

"I was just suggesting it!" Kris said.

POINT – Twin books always suggest feeding your babies as soon as you give birth. This is a lovely idea, and I'm sure it works wonderfully for many new mothers. My babies were 100% not interested. Cole screamed his head off, angry at the world. Ty stared quietly, studying our faces. We talked to them and hugged and kissed them and loved them, but there was no breastfeeding going on in that recovery room.

We called our families and a few friends to tell them we'd had two boys and their names. Though I felt great, I was itching horribly. I couldn't keep my hand away from scratching my nose. They had warned me that this was a side effect of the drugs. They said that they could give me some Benadryl to counteract the effect, but I didn't really want to take something that might make me sleepy. Even though Kris kept laughing at me and bringing attention to it, I could not keep from scratching and rubbing my nose. Kris was delighted.

"You look like a crack addict," he laughed.

"I can't help it!" I laughed back. With the hand that wasn't scratching, I held onto one nametagged baby, Kris the other, and we started our lives as a family.

Let the games begin.

10. You will not get tired of the attention you get with twins.

Books emphasize that you will tire of people asking you questions. Twins –even though they're not that rare – (2004, 2005, 2006 reports counted 32 twins per 1,000 live births) – generate a lot of interest. What's cuter than one baby? Two babies! Repeatedly, I read articles and heard advice on how annoying it was when strangers dared to ask you about them. A twin mom told me she didn't want to take them places when she was in a hurry due to people stopping her. There are lists of questions on the internet making fun of common and 'stupid' things people say to twin parents.

This was - and this is an understatement - not my experience.

Think of it this way. You just spent nine months creating two tiny, perfect human beings. You're the parent, so you think they're the greatest things in the world. You spend every waking hour - and many hours you wish you were sleeping – taking care of their needs. Of *course* they're fascinating and adorable! How could people *stop* from asking you about them?

First, though – the giant stomach. When you're pregnant with twins, it's usually pretty obvious that you're going to have more than one baby. People did ask me if I was having twins, or they asked when I was due. Neither question bothered me, because I looked full term at about five months. These people weren't blind - they were just curious. I'm a friendly person and didn't mind telling them I was having twins. I was so excited about it … I loved sharing the news. Ask me about my giant stomach!

No strangers ever inquired if I used fertility drugs, but they did ask the more polite question if twins ran in my family. Here's the facts about twins: most people don't know how twins work. They understand that there are identical and non-identical twins – but most can't immediately summon up the word 'fraternal.' Here's a quick summary: Fraternal twins occur when the woman releases two eggs and they're fertilized by two different sperm. Having fraternal twins can be genetic, in that a woman may be more genetically predisposed to releasing more than one egg. (The guy's genes have nothing to do with it.) Fertility drugs and older age of mothers also increase chances of releasing two eggs.

Identical twins occur when a fertilized egg splits. There's no hereditary trait that influences identical twins – at a very basic level, it's the malfunction of a normal development process (but with great results!) Identical twins don't run in families. The skipping a generation idea, which can be recited by most people, isn't true. Scientists don't know why the egg splits. Don't you love a medical mystery?

Therefore, when people asked, "Do twins run in your family?" The answer for me is no. There are a few sets of twins on Kris' side of the family, but his genes don't have anything to do with me shooting out two eggs at once. So I just say, "No, I just got lucky."

Once the babies were out and I took them everywhere with me, people often asked questions because it was hard not to notice us. You tend to notice a girl in the grocery store who has one infant car seat on the top of the cart and one in the basket. I never considered it intrusive or tiresome. I didn't often dress them alike (since a lot of their clothes were hand-me-downs) but it was obvious if someone looked that they were the same size and age.

I always thought it was so silly when mothers were reluctant to cut their baby boys' hair. However, I felt the same reluctance because I thought it was so cute. Attention from other people paid a role in this, when people started asking, “Are they twins? A boy and a girl?” Hint taken.

I notice other people’s twins and I would be surprised if people didn’t notice mine. Mothers always ask me and then tell me, “I had twins. They’re 42 now.” Once you have an eye for it, you can’t help it. But people notice babies and children, period. Wouldn’t it be a strange world if they didn’t?

&&&&

I know the appropriate things to say when someone's getting married, or a loved one has died. There are certain socially-acceptable things to say. I didn't know that there was an assigned phrase to say when you see someone with twins.

#1 most common phrase I heard was ... "You must have your hands full." Or "Don't you have your hands full!" or "Looks like you have your hands full." There are a couple variations, but one part is always the same - the phrase "hands full."

Kris commented that when people told me this, my hands were usually literally full - one car seat in each hand. But it wasn’t always true. People also said it when they were in a stroller or in a cart ... when I wasn’t even holding anyone. But it was still the knee-jerk response. I heard it at least once when I took them out. If I didn't, I'd probably begin to think something was wrong. Like I'd left one kid somewhere.

#2 coming in a distant second - "Oh, double trouble!"

There's nothing like rhyming that makes me smile. People didn't really expect a response other than that, so that worked out well for everyone involved. I mean, my babies didn't even move yet. How much trouble could they be?

Maybe they're thinking of later, when I'll need to be posting bond for two.

#3 "Are they twins?" People often make fun of themselves after asking this, but I don't think they should. Because in Alabama TWO women told me they "almost had twins." What did they mean? That they had two children within 12 months of each other. So, not a bad question at all. Even though we're in Michigan.

#4 most common among people helping me with them - "Am I putting them in the right side/seat?" My children didn't have assigned sides, seats, clothes, or even ... pacifiers. They're incredibly good at sharing. Because they don't even know they're sharing. But I appreciate people I'm hanging out with thinking that I'm actually able to keep track of who's supposed to be sitting where.

#5 nicest thing I heard. After all the "hands full" and "double trouble", I also from time to time hear kind comments, like "I always wanted twins". But the nicest comment came from a woman Kris and I sat next to on a plane.

First of all, I feel bad for people sitting next to us, because I always used to groan inwardly when seeing infants on a plane, knowing they were going to interrupt my sleep. (Haha! I had no clue what interrupted sleep was then, silly past-Carla!)

But when she sat down next to us, she looked at the babies and said with obvious pleasure, "Twins? Oh my goodness." She beamed at them and said brightly, "You just must be in heaven!"

I immediately teared up. She was right. Yes, my hands are full. Yes, I'll probably have trouble times two. Yes, someday they'll probably pretend not to be twins and fight over who owns what. But all of it - all of it - is exactly what I wished for.

Hands full? Yes. But a heart even more full.

&&&&

Basically, it's hard to get tired of hearing about how precious your children are. Right after I had them, Kris' aunt with twins told me, "I used to take the boys to the mall when I was feeling overwhelmed just to hear people tell me how beautiful they were and how lucky I was."

So if you're stuck at home with twins, maybe they need a change of scenery. Maybe you need to go soak up some compliments. Get out and show them off.

I'm waiting for the age when people don't pay attention to your kids anymore. I'm not certain what age that happens - seven? – but when it does, chances are people will still notice that you have two the same age. You get a kid-attention bonus!

Now, I've never actually been asked a rude question. 'Rude' questions on the internet included people asking, "Which one is older? Do you dress them alike? How can you tell them apart? And … "Are they twins?"

I personally don't think any of those are rude questions. I think they're common questions. How else are they going to know the answer if they asked? A rude question to me would be if a stranger asked if my body snapped back to normal after delivering twins. (I guess I don't go to places where they ask that. Gyms? Yoga studios? Plastic surgery waiting rooms?)

Two comments actually stick in my mind. Two weeks after I had the babies, a cashier asked me when I was due. I mumbled, "Soon," because I was too embarrassed to correct her. Two years later, a cashier asked questions about my boys and then hesitated. She looked at them and at me and said, "I just have to ask. Are they yours?"

"Yes!" I said, happy, thinking that she thought I was far too young and thin to have twins. She didn't explain. Maybe she just thought they didn't look like me. But I decided to go with my interpretation and not ask any follow-up questions that could potentially damage my boosted self-esteem.

So … enjoy! If you're in that much of a hurry that you can't hear about how cute your kids are … or you can't answer conversational questions … or you don't want to listen about twins someone else knows … then you're going to have trouble in going out whether you have twins or not.

11. Being pregnant lets you do things you wouldn't normally do.

When you're pregnant, you take better care of yourself. When you're tired, you sit down. You eat vegetables. You take vitamins. It doesn't seem that speeding really fast in your car would come into this equation, but for me, it certainly did.

Since I looked full term starting at about five months, I took this as my personal license to speed. I'm no stranger to tickets. I had seven speeding and violation tickets in the beginning of my driving career, none of them my fault, of course – but I've been ticket-free for over eight years now!

But once I got my huge stomach into my little Grand Prix, I felt liberated. I went over the speed limit, being an extremely cautious driver, because I knew if any policeman pulled me over, he would immediately think I was driving to the hospital. Especially if I were breathing hard and wiping my brow.

Some pregnant women don't like to drive. Or don't like to drive far from home. I considered it a get out of jail free card. Be safe, be careful, and enjoy going ten over!

&&&&

Besides being able to get places faster, being pregnant also allows you to play a role you wouldn't have otherwise …

I was in a bar with my husband Kris, his three college roommates, and one of their girlfriends – Kelly.

"Hey," Kelly said, "Isn't that Drew Stanton over there?"

We looked, and it was – outstanding Michigan State University quarterback Drew Stanton – recently graduated and entering the NFL draft the following weekend.

"Oh, I'm going to go get my picture taken with him," I said, maneuvering my 8-months-pregnant-with-twins stomach to get up from the table.

"Yeah, you should," Kris agreed. "Your mom will love that." She was a big fan.

Our friend Mike joked, "You should say something about the twins."

I walked up to Drew. He was surrounded with a bunch of friends, both guys and girls.

"Drew? Drew?" I said, tapping him on his giant bicep. He turned.

"We need to talk about this," I said, exaggeratedly pointing to my giant pregnant stomach.

While this in and of itself was mildly humorous, his reaction was what really made it funny.

All at once, he gasped in horror, grabbed his head with both hands, and jumped back from my stomach. His eyes may have popped out of his head. HE WAS TERRIFIED.

"Oh, I'm totally kidding!" I said quickly, hoping to restart his heart.

He tried to regain his composure as all of our friends - both his and mine - screamed with laughter. Everyone was laughing loud and long, and as his friends retold it to friends who didn't hear, the laughter would start again.

“That’s my husband over there!”I said in what I hoped was a reassuring manner. Kris paused to give a little wave with one hand while wiping tears with the other. “So … the draft is next weekend, right?” I said, thinking that a change of topic was in order.

“Um, yeah,” he said, smoothing his hair down. I think I spotted a patch that had spontaneously turned white. He was visibly still shaken.

“Can I get my picture taken with you?” I asked.

“Of course!” he said, obviously thankful that I was asking only for a picture and not child support.

We posed, arms around each other. I returned to my seat and they immediately left, his friends still laughing.

I went to work on Monday and told the story to 100-some coworkers at a staff meeting. I titled it ‘Fun Things to Do When You’re Pregnant’. People would come up and ask me to retell the story for months.

I like to imagine that Drew Stanton is retelling it somewhere too, as he uses birth control.

&&&&

One of the best things about being pregnant for me was also being able to eat whenever I wanted. Although it didn't always work out the best for me.

A month before I delivered, my stomach was very small, so I wasn't hungry a lot. However, I still had to eat to maintain my blood sugar level.

How did I know?

One day, I had some frozen yogurt and went for a little walk at after lunch. After work, I got groceries and decided to order a pizza from Pizza Hut for Kris and me.

While I waited the 15 minutes for the pizza, I went for a walk. It was a beautiful, sunny day, and I just wanted to be outside.

I returned, picked up the pizza, and got in the car.

Wow, I thought. I don't feel so hot. Maybe I better eat a piece of this pizza right now.

I picked a piece out of the box and took a bite.

I didn't want anyone coming in and out of the restaurant to be grossed out by this giant pregnant woman eating pizza IN HER CAR, so I started driving.

After I finished the first piece, I realized what time it was – 5:30pm. I hadn't eaten in almost four hours, and I'd been walking.

The babies were screaming for more fuel.

I finished the first piece, and my blood sugar still hadn't risen. Usually when this happens I can eat something like raisins, or drink some orange juice, and it's an immediate lift. Apparently it was going to happen a little more slowly with these complex carbohydrates!

As a result, I reached for piece number two.

Now, eating pizza at all is messy. Eating pizza in a car is doubly messy. Eating pizza while stopped at a stoplight, with cars surrounding you, when you KNOW you have tomato sauce on your cheeks is … just embarrassing. I was afraid to look around and really, really hoped that no one I knew was in the car beside me. I was the thing YouTube videos are made of – a giant girl stuffing her face with pizza IN HER CAR.

With piece number two gone, I got onto the highway stretch and realized I was only driving 45. My mind was sort of cloudy. I turned off the radio with the back of my hand – trying to avoid spreading the grease – and concentrated very hard on the road.

It still wasn't working. I was sweating profusely and my head hurt. I contemplated which would be better – pulling over and stopping, or making it home and lying down for a nap.

You know what would help? My mind whispered. Another piece of pizza.

I decided that little voice in my head was genius, and I ate pieces three and four with ease and aplomb. They were fantastic.

Of course, I never have any napkins in my car – because who eats in the car? – so I found a stray piece of tissue paper from a baby gift to wipe my face and hand. I stuck my hand up through my sun roof to try and blow off the grease.

I made it home, parked in the garage, and collapsed on the couch. I awoke 30 minutes later, feeling worlds better.

Kris came home. "What are you having for dinner?" he asked.

"You're having pizza," I told him, gesturing to the pizza on the counter.

"Really?!" he said, all excited. "What are you having?"

"I already had mine. To go," I said.

&&&&

Whenever you're feeling huge, try a drive, a joke, or pick up a pizza. Basically, try to enjoy all the benefits that a giant stomach can bring!

12. There's no manual for feeding your kids.

Everything I read said that babies should try rice cereal first. So when my babies were six months old, I fed them rice cereal mixed with formula. I thought they would be absolutely thrilled that they were eating something more filling than breastmilk or formula.

Neither of them liked it or expressed the least interest in eating it. I'd read that babies sometimes have to be introduced to a food ten times before they would eat it, so I wasn't giving up. But I tried the rice cereal myself and it tasted like metal. It was awful.

The next day, I fed them mushed up peas. They ate a ton. They loved it. I couldn't feed them fast enough.

So, for awhile, things were actually harder work. Not only was I nursing them, but I was feeding them as well. But it was necessary to fill them up. They were hungry, hungry boys.

But what I wanted was a manual. I wanted to know how many containers of mushed up baby food babies their age should be eating. I wanted numbers, sizes, charts – I wanted someone to tell me exactly how much and how often to feed them. I would ask other mothers and look on the internet to see how much they were supposed to be eating. It took me a long time to realize that this was ridiculous. Every person is different. Each person is going to need a different amount of food to be full.

Before I had kids, I was always amused by the phrase "good eater."

Look around you! I always wanted to say. Everyone gets good at eating eventually! Go to a Texas Roadhouse in Illinois on a Saturday night!

When my kids started eating food, it amused me even more. Because my kids ate like they were starving. I would alternate putting spoonfuls into their mouths and I could barely do it fast enough before they would cry for more.

When the boys were just over a year, I asked my brother, "How do I know how much to feed them?"

He sat quietly.

"You feed them until they stop eating," he said.

I could barely believe it. They ate so much – Cole in particular – that I would feed them until Ty stopped and Cole slowed down.

When they finally could pick up their own food, I was thrilled. Finally – they could feed themselves as much as they wanted.

This ushered in an era of meals that lasted at least an hour. Breakfast, lunch, dinner – they would eat continually for an hour. They would pick up whatever food I put on their trays – many different courses – and eat it.

I asked my friend Moriah, "How long do they eat for an hour?"

She stared at me. "Not very long, I guess, because I don't remember that happening."

Then one day, they – collectively, since they work as a team – didn't want a lot of the food I put in front of them. They all of a sudden didn't like broccoli or peas.

So I put the vegetables in yogurt or applesauce. Again, they loved them. I mean, who doesn't love their vegetables covered in dairy or fruit?! It seemed gross, but I wanted them to eat healthy food.

Then suddenly, Cole decided he didn't like meat. I tried the meat in the applesauce trick again, but he could amazingly remove every particle of applesauce and spit out a perfectly clean piece of meat. Like an owl pellet.

Then he decided he didn't like oatmeal. Or Cheerios. Or bread. Or a whole list of things. He became one of those toddlers that you don't understand how they're surviving on so little food. I was determined not to let him consume only fruit and milk. I envisioned Cole becoming a picky eater like Kris and me.

One night when he was two I made spaghetti – which he had eaten and liked in the past - and I dished up the hamburger with spaghetti sauce on it for the boys. Ty spooned it up and ate merrily away. Cole cried. I tried to give him a spoonful but he twisted away and threw himself as far away from the spoon as possible.

I thought of the story my friend Amy told me: "I was at a restaurant and I saw this family with a three-year-old and he was eating sushi and vegetables. And I thought, 'I have white-trashed my child's diet. All he eats is chicken fingers and French fries.' Don't make that mistake."

Not that spaghetti is gourmet food … but I wanted him to at least TRY different foods. Even if he wasn't that willing.

So while Cole was crying, I grabbed some of the hamburger and stuffed it into his mouth.

He chewed it, prepared to spit it out and be furious, but instead immediately picked up his spoon and dug in. After awhile, he stopped using his spoon and just started shoving giant handfuls of meat into his mouth. He ate three bowls.

He might not ever like sushi, but someday he'll fit right in at the Texas Roadhouse.

&&&&

My boys ate and now will eat anything. They want new foods all the time. They ask, "Something new. Something different."

They're asking a girl who has eaten the same foods for over a decade. But I try to appease them. I give them every vegetable and fruit. They eat things I would never eat, like pickles and meatloaf.

Everyone makes jokes, because at three years old they'd eat two sloppy joes each for dinner. And side dishes. They said, "Just wait until they're teenagers."

And as a I filled my grocery carts, I thought, it's okay. At least they eat and aren't afraid to try new foods.

I've seen some little girls who don't eat very much food at all. They just aren't hungry. I feed my kids cereal, peanut butter toast and fruit for breakfast so that they don't start asking to eat again until 10:30am. They're just hungry kids.

Of course, some people would think that I feed my kids differently. I don't feed them chips or crackers. I don't feed them fruit snacks or candy. I don't have them on a low-fat diet by any means - they just snack on things like cheese or fruit or cereal. It would be a lot easier to feed them packaged snacks, don't get me wrong. We just don't have those things around.

So – don't worry about how much to feed your kids. If they act hungry, feed them. If they aren't hungry, don't feed them. And most importantly, if you want something to eat only by yourself, go and hide in the kitchen to eat it. It's impossible to eat without sharing around here.

13. Potty training might not require a steam cleaner.

I didn't look forward to potty training my boys. I didn't even own a steam cleaner. And we got new carpet before they were born. The idea of pee or poop on my carpet was very distasteful. Keeping them corralled in only tiled or hardwood areas – like a dog – was out of the question too. (Not on principle, but because we had large doorways unsuited for baby gates.)

I read up on it and learned that boys are harder to potty train and waiting until they were three-years-old might make it easier. This seemed like a great plan to me. First of all, changing diapers was not at all a big deal. Before my babies were born, I'd changed perhaps ten diapers in my life. Kris had changed exactly one. But we learned very quickly how to do it easily and efficiently. The boys didn't use that many diapers, either. Sure, I changed them every time they pooped, but that was once a day. So at age two, most days I used three diapers per child.

I want you to take note of that. I've read some statistics on how many diapers people used for twins and was baffled. It wasn't just starting at age two - during *most* of age two, we used three diapers a day. I don't know if my kids go less than other kids or if other people just change them more. We never had a problem with diaper rash or anything. I'm guessing that other children poop more than once a day. I don't know how to make this happen. I'm just saying that not every child needs eight diapers a day. Thankfully!

So, six diapers a day total? Only two poopy? At my pro level? At that point, changing diapers seemed way easier than potty training.

However, my friends were potty training their two-year-olds with some success. My mom mentioned my neighbor, who had apparently potty trained all of her grandchildren. Her method took one day.

I gave her a call. Did she potty train them at age three?

"Some of them I did … but I prefer training them at age two," she told me. "Once they use the potty and understand what it's for, don't use diapers again," she counseled.

"But what about in public?" I asked.

"They're even more conscious of it in public. They're less likely to pee their pants in public than they are at home," she said. She added, "And it's easier to do it in the summer when you're likely to be outside."

I borrowed a friend's potty and had one of my own. I put them both in the bathroom next to the toilet. I showed them to the boys and talked about how their friends used them and had them sit on them. They had a little interest, but not much.

I left the potties in the bathroom and they ignored them for the next week.

The three of us were swimming in the pool together in June, right after the boys turned two years old. They were swimming without swimsuits. Ty got out of the pool and looked down at the water dripping off of him. He said, "I want the potty. Go get it."

"Okay …" I said. I brought the potty and two cups of water outside. Ty sat on the potty and peed in it. I made a huge deal. Cole did it too. I made a huge deal. I gave them multiple cups of water and they continued to drink and pee on the potty for the rest of the day.

That night, I bought underwear at the store. After they woke up the next morning, I told them they were going on the potty and wearing underwear – no more diapers.

Oh, they were all about it. They were super excited at the whole underwear and potty experience. Since it was summer and we were outside a lot, I took one of the potties outside with us so we wouldn't have to truck all the way indoors.

They did a great job. They weren't capable of pulling down or up their pants and underwear, so that was my part of the job. But it was preferable to changing diapers.

The first time a boy pooped his pants we were outside and I washed his underwear with the hose. The second time, same thing. The third time, I was between clothing changes and they both pooped in the yard, with relatives over. Who kindly pretended not to notice that I was picking up after my children with a plastic bag over my hand.

As for pee … my kids never peed in my house. One of them peed in my mom's house twice during the potty training. I felt bad, but was also glad it wasn't at my house. (It wasn't on her carpet, thank goodness.)

Another time a boy pooped on my bathroom floor as he waited for the other boy to go on the toilet. I considered that one sort of my fault. He obviously needed to go first. A challenge in a house with only one toilet! Even for the well-potty trained among us! That's what you get for living in an old house that has no place you can put another toilet unless it's an outhouse. Which I sometimes consider.

I was nervous about taking them out in public, but I would just ask them to go before we left the house. They were really good about it. They also have amazing bladder control. Even at age three, they only went to the bathroom three or four times a day. I go that many times before 8am. Still, to go out in public I always took another two sets of pants and underwear, just in case.

By a month, they were potty trained well enough that I didn't worry about them. My carpet was feces and urine free. Glorious!

Eventually, the potty just seemed a little small for them. They had a step they could use to get up to the real toilet. Eventually they could remove their pants, climb up, and sit on the potty. Move the step over, and wash their hands. It was a long motor skills process, and I still had to help them redress a lot, but overall the transition went quite well.

I should mention – I taught them to go sitting down. My dad babysat them one day and said, "No wonder they were confused when I helped them go to the bathroom!" I thought it was easier to teach them while sitting until they were tall enough to reach the toilet.

I put them in diapers or pull-ups while they slept for a long time, until they woke up dry, a little before they turned three years old. (This only seemed fair to them. They couldn't climb out of their cribs, go downstairs, remove their footie pajamas, and go potty during the night. And I didn't really want them waking me up. So they slept in diapers until they could make it 12 hours.) It didn't happen at exactly the same time, seeing as how they are different people. With different bladders.

So potty training was not the scary nightmare I was expecting. Once they understood, and once they were in underwear, they got it. I think the transition and then never turning back (while awake) made it clear to them.

I understand the rewarding them with food or treats or bribes would also work. My kids didn't require this, because the act of doing something new was enough for them. Plus, they wanted to do it, which makes a big difference.

Experts also counsel that you should not yell at your kids when they go in their pants. I adhered to this for a little while … until they knew better. I didn't want to scare them in the beginning, but once I knew that they knew what was going on, I would tell them I was disappointed in them and show my displeasure.

So … cold turkey on the diapers, stressing understanding, being firm, and no steam cleaner. Another hurdle cleared in the process of helping your babies grow up. Or at least be cleared to enter preschool.

14. What other people need isn't necessarily what you need.

I got a lot of other mothers' advice when I was pregnant, and looked at a lot of other mothers' registries. Wonderful family members and friends threw me great showers, and I had gifts galore. I felt so ready to have my babies.

At work, some friends made me a diaper cake, with many, many little, light baby blankets. Various shapes, sizes, colors, all the same material. (I found out later they had a name - receiving blankets.)

As I folded them and tried to find room for them, I laughed to myself. Who on earth would need this many blankets?

After I had the babies, I realized the gift-givers knew more than I did.

I used those blankets for everything. Wrapped babies. Cleaned up spit up. Laid them down to change diapers. Used as a sunshade in the car seat. Threw over self to nurse. Laundered them – because I *always needed more.*

I don't recall seeing a blanket like this before I had children (but of course people had them.) I don't remember anyone telling me that I'd want to own 45 small blankets. I found them incredibly useful.

On the flip side, you don't always need what other people do.

For instance, a Boppy. I thought they looked awesome for nursing, and people loved to sit their babies in them. It made perfect sense. Just because I couldn't nurse with them (I was the wrong shape, or it was the wrong position, or something – I just didn't like it) and my babies didn't like to sit in them, doesn't mean that millions of people are wrong. They're not wrong. You just never know what you want until you're in the moment. With crying, hungry babies.

Another item I registered for was a sheet saver. This is a thin piece of material (about baby-sized) that you tie onto your sheet so it doesn't move. You lay your baby on it so that you don't have to strip the entire bed – just take that off and replace it with another one.

I didn't see the point of this with twins. First of all, when they were in bed together, I'd need two of them. And they moved around a lot. The sheet saver and the babies.

And I didn't see the difficulty in taking off a sheet and washing it. Now, truthfully, I didn't have any additional bedding – no bumpers or frilly things on the crib or anything additional like that. So taking a sheet off a bed wasn't a big deal. Instead, it was … exactly like washing a sheet saver. But in theory they sounded like a great idea!

The baby Bumbo seats came to my attention when my babies were about six months old. I thought they were fantastic. I ordered one online – even though it seemed a little bit pricey, I thought it would be great for them! They could sit up in a little mini-armchair! Right next to me! And be entertained! I could feed them in it! Etc. We got it in the mail and I excitedly opened it and displayed it to my kids. I put Cole in it first, but … his legs were too fat. I really had to cram his little (giant) things in between the unforgiving plastic. Hmm. I guess it wasn't the best for him. I put Ty in it. He tolerated it for a little while, but really disliked not being able to move his legs, since they were immobilized. I took him out and thought about reselling the Bumbo online as soon as possible. Soon after, the news came out with Bumbo warnings not to put the chair anywhere on a counter, table, high up places, where the baby could get himself out of it and fall off. I hadn't even thought of that. As I got ready for church one Sunday morning, instead of having Cole cry on my feet like normal, wondering why I wasn't holding him for the five minutes it took to do my hair and makeup, I put him in the Bumbo on the sink. He was much happier being able to see what I was doing. I didn't go more than a few inches away from him, because I already knew the warnings. So they were a good five minutes we had, the Bumbo and me. It went into my parents' basement along with other things I hope to sell someday.

Onto bottles. Since I gave my babies a bottle a day, I didn't really experiment with bottles. I had three bottles, and I washed them in the dishwasher each night after they used them. I encouraged the babies to hold their own bottles as soon as possible. I would prop their little hands up and try to get them to hold onto them, even if it was only by accident. They could, pretty early, which was helpful to me. However, their bottles leaked on them. Apparently Ty, in particular, couldn't drink as fast as the bottle released liquid.

Sometimes he would have it all down his neck. It was gross. Until he learned to drink faster – or to never pause – he would have milk on him. Later, when they could hold their bottles firmly and remove them, smile, and return to drinking, they would be soaked. Anytime they stopped, the bottle would just sort of trickle onto them.

Why didn't I get new bottles? Did I think that all bottles would be like that? Apparently. Because they had the same three bottles the entire year they drank from them.

Soon after I had my kids, I saw pictures of another twin mom's kids … with bottles with detachable nipples. So you don't have to hold the bottle at all. The bottle sits upright, and a tube with the bottle's nipple on it goes in the baby's mouth. (One brand name is the Podee Handsfree Feeding System.) So you can easily feed two babies at once without holding them. If only I'd seen them a year earlier! Ty's neck fold would have required a lot less attention.

Another item I registered for and never needed were sippy cups. I understand why people like sippy cups, especially for traveling. You don't want your kids to spill liquid everywhere. I registered for two nice sippy cups with handles. The day after my boys turned one year old I put away their bottles and handed them sippy cups. They were intrigued, but had difficulty getting any liquid out of them. I tried it – and it was hard! You really had to put forth some serious suction to get anything out of there! So I removed the plastic plug in the cup that created the suction. Then it was just a cup with a hole. They could drink out of that … but it was a really small hole. I did that for a couple of days and then just started giving them regular cups of milk. It was so much easier for them to actually consume liquid that way.

Of course, for walking around the house, this would never work. But I never did that. They could drink while they were eating or they could drink on the kitchen rug, and other than that they never had liquid. They still don't. (Truthfully, neither do we, so it's not an issue of them trying to copy us.) Like I said, I don't own a steam cleaner. And we all know that sour milk and carpet is a horrible combination.

There are other items on checklists that I never needed and think you can pass on until you actually HAVE the baby and decide that it's necessary. My sister warned me against getting a diaper pail. They take special garbage bags and they fill up really quickly, she said. It's not really that much more work to put a diaper in a garbage can away from your living quarters.

Rectal thermometers. Every checklist I see for babies has a rectal thermometer on it. I never took my babies' temperature rectally. I'm pretty sure I wouldn't even be able to bring myself to do it. What does a sick baby love more than anything? Having a foreign object shoved up its butt? I don't think so. There are so many more ways to check a temperature … they have the ear thermometer, the forehead strips, the good old mouth thermometer … I would pretty much pick anyway other than rectally. If you think a baby has a fever - and I know it's hard to trust yourself now – your baby has a fever. The age-old way of feeling his forehead works. He'll be hot. He'll be listless. He'll feel crummy and look awful. He has a fever.

Onesies. Onesies are a great idea … for a time. For instance, my babies spent most of June, July, and August in onesies. Because it was hot, and our house doesn't have air conditioning. They were perfect for that. Later, there seems to be no point to them. Because do you know what attracts poop more that cloth put RIGHT NEXT TO A DIAPER? Nothing. I would often see other parents put a onesie on a child – and then more clothes over it! So then if a kid gets poop or pee on the onesie, you have to take everything off and replace it. It is making having a kid in diapers way harder than it would be otherwise. Why? Is it important that a baby looks like his shirt is tucked in, just in case he scores a job interview on the way home from the grocery store? Just a onesie – yes. Onesie plus clothes – no. This goes for when they're older as well. I was seeing onesies in 3T sizes. It's really hard to have a kid unsnap his own clothes to go to the bathroom. It's way easier to pull down pants – in diapers or not – rather than unsnap and snap clothes. There's a reason adults don't wear them. (Well, I'm guessing here. I guess if someone has a onesie on under their clothes, I just don't know about it.)

Breastpump. I bought an expensive double breast pump. Brand name and all. Pretty top of the line. It wasn't as good as the commercial-grade pump at the hospital, but it was good. But any breastpump, in my experience, can't compare to a baby. Babies, when they get it, are good at nursing. They get out *way* more than a breastpump. So you feed a baby, and you want to pump, and you just cannot get out as much as you know, deep in your heart, that your baby is getting. Not that it's not necessary – I pumped for my Cole when he was in the NICU. I pumped when I was going away from them. But not a ton. I didn't like the breastpump. I felt like it was only sort of working. I admire women who are able to pump for their babies. I realize it works – we do have a dairy farm and all, so pumps working on lactating cows are how we make our money – but I didn't enjoy it.

Not only that, but it messed with my mind. The whooshing of the motor made sounds like it was talking to me. The first time after it happened I immediately googled it and was rewarded with an entire site of women talking about what their pump was saying to them. That made me feel better.

I'm not saying that if you're nursing you're not going to need a pump. I'm saying you might need different kinds for different reasons. For instance, when my babies were seven months old, I went to Phoenix for a weekend for a bachelorette party. Since I was still nursing them, I took my breast pump to keep up my milk production while I was away.

I didn't think it was a big deal … I'd just pump every few hours just like I fed the boys. The first day, I needed to pump. It would have been painful not to do it. The second day, my milk production started lagging. It was a lot harder to produce milk. I had to use all my concentration to let my milk down. The third day, I *had* to pump, or it would have stopped completely, it felt like. And it was in this frame of mind that I was flying home.

I was going through the Minneapolis airport and wanted to use my pump, which I'd packed in my carryon. I then found that – airports don't have outlets in their stalls.

That's okay, I thought. I don't mind horribly if I have to do it in the general area of the restroom.

Except – there weren't any outlets in the general area either. I supposed I'd never needed one before and just assumed they would be along the sink … like they are in most places. But no.

I asked an airport employee if there was anywhere I could use a breastpump. She instructed me to walk to a private, handicapped restroom several gates away. Since I had the time, I didn't mind the 20 minute walk there, but I was glad I wasn't rushing to my connection.

I entered the single bathroom – labeled 'medical assistance' - and was happy to plug in my pump. Only – as soon as I let go of the plug, my pump stopped. I fiddled around with the cord, getting a little anxious, and found that if I held the plug in the outlet with one hand, and kept the other hand on me, then I could manipulate it to be at *just* the right angle so that it would work and I could express milk. This meant I could only do one breast at a time, but I settled in and figured it was better than nothing.

That's when the knocking started. "Cleaning crew!" I heard.

"I'm in here!" I yelled back. "Occupied!"

The knocking didn't stop the entire time I was pumping. Three separate times, the cleaning crew knocked and told me through the door, more agitated and annoyed each time, that they were ready to clean my bathroom *right now.*

When I finished, quicker than I would have liked and more harried than before, I exited the bathroom to a see a cleaning crew of three people sitting, staring at me, wondering why I took so long. When I got home to my little babies a few hours later, I was so excited to see them and thought they'd be so excited to see me and nurse. They were happy to see me … but had almost zero interest in nursing. I sort of had to force them. They were just a little bit more willing than that pump.

After telling this story to a friend, she told me I needed something I didn't even (yet) realize existed. A hand pump. With a hand pump, I could skip packing the cords, the battery pack, the bottles … for milk I was just pouring out. I could skip the extended walk and irritated employees and barely functional electrical systems. As an added bonus, I could pump while sitting in a regular stall. So I'm not saying that you don't need a breast pump. I'm saying it might be beneficial to have more than one kind. Happy registering!

15. There are things you do with single babies you just don't do with twins.

When my twins were three years and four months old, I had a single baby – a boy we named Max. The boys couldn't have been more welcoming and loving. It was a pleasant surprise. I thought that perhaps since they were used to sharing attention already, this wasn't the life-changing experience that many older children have. He quickly moved into our family's routine and hearts.

When you have a single baby, you do things you wouldn't do when you have two at a time.

Sleep with a baby on your chest.

By the time Max was one month old, I'd already lost count of the times he slept on my chest. Why? Because my twins took a nap from 1-3pm. If Max wasn't tired or was fussy during those hours … it meant I wasn't going to get a nap.

And I wanted one! I was tired! So he slept on my chest sometimes. Why didn't I do this with twins? Because with them I felt like I'd be favoring one over the other.

Wear a front pack every day.

I spent a lot of time alone with the twins. As a result, I wasn't going to wear one child and leave the other. With three children, I still needed two in the stroller, so wearing the third seemed like an easy option. I spent a lot of time with Max in the front pack outside. Kris would wear him when he needed to do things like make dinner – and Max didn't want to be put down.

Nurse the baby whenever he feels like it.

Since I nursed the boys in tandem, it sort of felt like a production. I didn't even use any props, but just the act of nursing them together made it seem like I was doing something that required … planning. With a single baby, anytime he acts hungry I fed him. I'd read about cluster feedings, and Max was certainly hungry more often at certain times – sometimes wanting to eat every hour. And what did I do? I fed him! I had enough milk, I wasn't that sore, it made him happy, it made me happy to have him content …

if the boys wanted to eat any more than often than every 2.5 hours, I would just try to stave them off. And if one wanted to eat and the other one didn't? It didn't matter – they were eating together!

Wear nursing pads.

I didn't understand nursing pads before I had one baby. What was the point? I never leaked milk. Then I had one baby … and I got it. I had an excess. I never had any extra when I was nursing twins. Suddenly, these were very important items in my house! And for my clothes!

Use a million diapers.

When I had just twins, they simply didn't use a lot of diapers. Perhaps they weren't getting as much food. Maybe it was because they started out much smaller and took their time growing. (To compare, Max was 30% bigger than each of them at birth.) As a result, I was surprised that when I changed his diaper in the first month – about eight times a day – he had pooped almost every time. I then understood why people talked about using that many diapers. Some kids poop a lot, some kids don't. For the first month of their lives, I think single Max used as many as the two of them did together.

Fit into your clothes.

When I was pregnant with the twins, I gained 45 pounds. When I was pregnant with Max, I gained 18 pounds. This wasn't on purpose – I just wasn't hungry. Obviously, just mathematically, it's easier to lose the weight when you have less to lose. Even when you think your jeans will fit, every pair of mine hit the incision line dead on. After about six weeks it didn't bother me as much. Even though it still didn't feel great, I'd have done about anything to stop wearing maternity pants.

Let him set his own schedule.

Max duped me. For the first month, he didn't cry. He was happy when he was awake, he would eat and go back to sleep happily, he was a really content baby.

Then, when he hit the month mark, he was unhappy. He cried and fussed in the evenings, he wanted to be held all the time, he didn't want to go back to sleep at night after he ate. He just wanted to be held, patted, and comforted.

"He fooled us!" I declared to Kris.

On one hand, this was good news for me. When he was so happy, I thought – that's it. I was starving my twins. They were crying because they were STARVING and why didn't I just feed them formula!? Why did I torture them so?!

But when Max started acting exactly like them – crying, fussing, etc. – I was glad. There was no way he was starving. Instead, I just have BABIES THAT CRY.

I couldn't help being a little bit happy, and tried to wait patiently for when he would start talking and tell me what he wanted. Hooray!

By two months, he was sleeping through the night. Since I'd had the twins, I'd been convinced that people who said their kids slept through the night that early were lying. I told myself each night, "Don't get used to it. Don't get used to sleeping." And each night he'd go to sleep and sleep seven, eight, even nine hours. I was amazed. When he did wake up on a rare night after only six hours, I'd drag myself into his room, feed him … and he'd go immediately back to sleep. I realized why some people have 12 kids. Because they have babies like this.

When he was almost four months, he started waking up every three hours to eat. He didn't want comforting … he really was hungry, ramming his little head into me to let me know what he wanted. I expected at nine months he'd start sleeping through the night for good … just like his big brothers.

&&&&

Really, what I want to tell twin moms is this: don't be afraid. You're just the next in a long line of mothers taking care of two babies at a time. It's not easy all the time, but it is wonderful. Your kids will like each other. They always have a playmate and someone their age who thinks they're hilarious. (My kids are laughing at each other all the time! At things that aren't, to the outsider, super funny!) You automatically have a family – or if they're not your first kids – a big family. You'll rarely be bored. Life with twins, after about six weeks, is the pretty much the same as having two kids any age.

So, enjoy yourself. Hold your crying babies tight. Laugh at your two toddlers. Be happy when your little babies grow up to be big brothers – and are really good at it.

Just recently I was at the grocery store with all three boys. Ty and Cole were sitting in the top of the racecar grocery cart steering us around, and Max was in his car seat in the basket.

"Ooh, you look like you have your hands full," a man said to me. "How close are they in age?"

"They're twins," I said.

"Hey, better you than me!" he laughed.

I laughed too. I guessed so! I consider myself incredibly lucky to have twins. And if you picked up this book – congrats to you too. It looks like you're going to have your hands full. In the best way possible.